TO PLAY OR NOT TO PLAY

is it really a question?

Christine Jeandheur Ferguson
and
Ernest Dettore, Jr.,
Editors

Association for Childhood Education International
17904 Georgia Ave., Ste. 215, Olney, MD, 20832
www.acei.org • 800-423-3563

Bruce Herzig, ACEI Editor
Anne Bauer, ACEI Editor
Deborah Jordan Kravitz, Production

Copyright (c) 2007, Association for Childhood Education International
17904 Georgia Ave., Ste. 215, Olney MD 20832

Library of Congress Cataloging-in-Publication Data

To play or not to play : is it really a question? / Christine Jeandheur Ferguson and Ernest Dettore, Jr., editors.
    p. cm.
 Includes bibliographical references.
 ISBN 978-0-87173-170-8 (pbk.)
 1. Play. 2. Early childhood education--Philosophy. 3. Child development. I. Ferguson, Christine Jeandheur. II. Dettore, Ernest.

LB1137.T585 2007

                                                      155.41'8--dc22
                                                      2006038893

TABLE OF CONTENTS

"To be or not to be: that is the question."

Shakespeare, *Hamlet*

This powerful quote from Shakespeare's *Hamlet* poses the question as to whether Hamlet should continue living or not. *"To exist or not to exist, that's the question for me"* paraphrases his dilemma. This is a profound question asked at a time of peril. The essence of the question defines the focus of "To Play or Not To Play: Is It Really a Question?" During a time in our education system when play is being assaulted from many fronts, we, too, find a climate of peril; play is in danger. Play, once commonplace in classrooms, is now found only outside the classroom. Now, we are finding play removed from outside the classroom by the elimination of recess. Where is the place for play? Where will it exist, so our children can *flourish*? The resounding call for play's existence issues from courageous people willing to demand that play live, that play exist. To live or not to live? To exist or not to exist? To be or not to be? To play or not to play? Are these really valid questions when the stakes are so high, the alternative so bleak? This book takes the necessary step in affirming play's vital role in child development and provides a voice for play. To play or not to play? No, it should not be in question!

In the first chapter, *Play and the Brain*, Bergen investigates play and brain development. First, she investigates what we know about play and why people play. Next, Bergen looks at play's role in brain development, based on scientific explorations of brain activity. In looking at the brain's structures, functions, and development, the complexities of the brain emerge and the role of play in promoting the brain's development can be explored. Bergen hypothesizes about play and brain connections. Even though more neuropsychological research is needed, play development and brain development appear to have many parallels. Bergen proposes that enhancing play opportunities most likely is useful in helping the brain develop as well. Bergen recognizes that play is rarely included in the school curriculum because it is seen as unimportant or meaningless. Perhaps as brain research offers more evidence of play and brain connections, play will be more valued by the school community. Until that time, Bergen strongly supports the pursuit of play and its role in enriching brain development.

Chapter 2 focuses on the increased mobility of people throughout world and the growing number of culturally and linguistically diverse children in our classrooms. Because of this phenomenon, Szecsi and Giambo recognize the importance of educators creating a culturally and linguistically responsive curriculum by becoming aware of diverse play patterns across cultures. They offer a sampling of playful experiences within cultural contexts of play initiated by children, parents, and teachers from cultures outside the United States. The experiences illuminate the unique cultural and linguistic features, as well as the benefits, of play. The chapter also provides insight into how play can facilitate children's cultural and linguistic competencies. For example, Szecsi and Giambo highlight play's role in helping children construct their identity, racial awareness, social and cultural norms, native language, and acceptance of other cultures. The international examples provide awareness of culturally specific play experiences, thus leading educators to enhance play environments so that we can embrace our culturally and linguistically diverse children in our classrooms.

Dettore investigates the value and contribution of play in Chapter 3. He delivers a strong case for play in a world where play is slowly disappearing. Dettore discusses the reasons for the absence of play and how societal trends have undermined childhood. For example, television and computers steal children's playtime, parents overschedule children in a variety of programs, and educational trends have marginalized play. Society is focused more on academic achievement through standards and testing, to the point that the existence of play is in jeopardy. Dettore gives a dramatic view of a lost world of play, but ascertains that if society acted on the knowledge and research about play, then play would be protected and cherished in all of society (Seefeldt, 1995).

Ferguson defines sociodramatic play in Chapter 4. She explores the value of sociodramatic play, the relationship between sociodramatic play and literacy learning, how to establish a play-based curriculum that can promote literacy development, and how to involve children in constructing sociodramatic play. Sociodramatic play impacts a child's development of abstract thought, language, social skills, and acquisition of knowledge. Children even express their emotions through sociodramatic play. Ferguson aptly describes these benefits of sociodramatic play and then focuses on the significant relationship between sociodramatic play and literacy development. Research shows that literacy-enriched play environments enhance literate behaviors. Yet, as Ferguson laments, the obvious benefits of sociodramatic play have been largely ignored, and the push for academics negatively impacts the chances to implement a play-based curriculum for young children. She then gives a detailed example of how children can be valuable contributors to sociodramatic play when encouraged to express their interests and real-life experiences. The pet theme vividly portrays children's emerging literacy through play. Ferguson strongly demonstrates that academics are not lost, but rather enhanced, through play.

Chapter 5 asserts that play is an essential tool for children's social competence and identity development. This chapter identifies some of the ways in which children shape their social and cultural identities through play. McNulty focuses on the power of early play experiences, the development of gender-role stereotypes, understanding of culture, and the role of the media in children's play. She continually reminds us of the important role of the adults in children's lives; we can support and protect play for children in relationship to their social and cultural identities, or we can endorse stereotypes by criticism or neglect and stifle imagination and experimentation.

Booth, Ehrlich, and Deasy look at the arts and play in Chapter 6. The authors attest to the positive impact early art experiences have on children's learning and development. Art supports brain connections, strengthens imagination, refines cognitive and creativity skills, and supports critical thinking skills. Art is play for young children, a place for fantasy, and a source of joy and wonder. The authors emphasize the important role of educators in supporting art in the classroom and offer specific ways educators can provide for exploration of the arts and play. They, too, recognize the barriers that exist to limit the role of arts in education, and cite the shift toward academic standards, and the lack of arts-oriented professional development and funding. A narrow definition of schooling leads to less time for children to engage in play and the arts. The authors call for greater attention to the *necessity* of arts education; art is not a frill.

Chapter 7 examines the literature on play and the special needs child. Mastrangelo and Killoran uncover the reality that children with disabilities often experience play deprivation and feelings of incompetence. The conflict between their internal drive to play and their inability to access play can lead to learned helplessness, thus decreasing children's self-esteem. Unfortunately, play is not considered important enough to include on children's IEPs, because the focus is on academic development. There is a conflict between those who adhere to more traditional methods of direct instruction, and those who understand the power of play. The authors emphasize the importance for adults to find ways to incorporate play into special needs children's daily experiences. They offer possibilities among the challenges. Mastrangelo and Killoran outline the important benefits of play for children with disabilities and give guidelines on how to incorporate play into an IEP. Without preparation, children with disabilities may not have the opportunity to experience play. By making provisions for play, children with disabilities can flourish.

In Chapter 8, by Kathleen Burriss, proposes the extended benefits for children's development through outdoor play. As she notes, play should not be used as a reward because the "real work" of school is done. Burriss discusses guidelines for both free and guided forms of outdoor play and how to create playscapes for all children. She underscores the importance for adults to be aware of, and plan for, outdoor play. Burriss also asks the question, "What is the future of outdoor learning and play?" Limited understanding, diminished funds, and restricted space threaten the existence of outdoor play. She laments how our hurried society and children's after-school schedules leave little or no time for outdoor play, but encourages us to step forward, "with one step, then another," and begin the venture.

"To play or not to play? Is it really a question?" The authors answer this profound query with powerful examples of the importance of play for our children. However, they also see the danger, the dark cloud obscuring the vision for our children's well-being supported through play. Fortunately, in this book, "play" loudly calls for its place of existence, *to be,* and passionately voices its strong will—to continue to live in the lives of children everywhere. To play or not to play? We answer the question with a resounding "yes," but realize we also have a solemn responsibility to protect and promote play for the sake of our children. To live, to exist, to play, to *flourish*!

ACKNOWLEDGMENTS

Many people were instrumental in helping us write this book. To begin, we acknowledge our own teachers and colleagues, who inspired us to think creatively and become true advocates for childhood play. Mac Brown, University of South Carolina; Tom Reed, University of South Carolina Upstate; Fred Rogers of "Mister Rogers" fame; Horton Southworth, Emeritus Professor, University of Pittsburgh; and Mark McKenna have all been mentors and role models who continued to challenge us and advance our quest for knowledge about the value of play.

Special thanks to the children in our classrooms and our lives (our own children and grandchildren) who have also been, in a sense, our teachers. They have provided us with observational experiences of the social and educational nature of play. Moreover, they have encouraged us to think beyond the realms of observing children's play as just a frivolous activity, but truly enabled us to acknowledge the many benefits of childhood play in development and learning.

We are particularly indebted to the following friends and authors who supported and helped us write this book: Doris Bergen, Miami University; Howard Booth, Elizabeth Deasy, and Linda Ehrlich, Shady Lane School; Kathleen G. Burriss, Middle Tennessee State University; Debra A. Giambo and Tunde Szecsi, Florida Gulf Coast University; Isabel Killoran, York University; Sonia Mastrangelo, doctoral candidate at York University; Carol McNulty, University of North Carolina at Wilmington; and Sandra Stone, Northern Arizona University.

We also thank the reviewers for their comments on and suggestions for this book: Wendy Dover, Fort Mill School District; Bradley S. Witzel, Winthrop University; Emie Tittnich, University of Pittsburgh, Office of Child Development, and Elke Schneider, Winthrop University.

Additionally, we thank our spouses—husband, Dane Ferguson, and wife, Cathy Dettore, respectively—who supported and encouraged us to pursue this important endeavor in promoting the value of childhood play.

Lastly, we extend our heartfelt thanks to Anne Bauer, Bruce Herzig, and Deborah Jordan Kravitz, editorial staff at the Association for Childhood Education International, for their time, patience, support, expertise, and efforts in assisting us in the completion and publication of this book.

—**Christine Jeandheur Ferguson and Ernest Dettore, Jr.**

P lay is a phenomenon that has been of interest to theorists and researchers for over a century. It has been defined in many ways and its purpose and value have been examined and debated. Play also has been the subject of numerous books for teachers and parents. Although a variety of play's aspects have been hypothesized as being related to children's development of physical, cognitive, language, and social-emotional skills, it is only recently that these hypotheses can be investigated as part of the study of brain development. This chapter explores what is presently known, as well as what may be known in the future, regarding play and the brain.

What Do We Know About Play?

In the past 100 years, many writers have attempted to define play, and their definitions have been varied, including:

- The natural unfolding of the germinal leaves of childhood (Froebel)
- Activities not consciously performed for the sake of any result beyond themselves (Dewey)
- The aimless expenditure of exuberant energy (Schiller)
- The basic foundation of human culture (Huizinga)
- A requirement for the evolution of mammals (Ellis, 1998, p. 29)
- A dispositional factor (Rubin).

(See Spodek & Saracho, 1998, for further discussion of these and other play definitions.)

Although the definitions vary in emphasis, one thing that seems certain is that both adults and children can distinguish playful from nonplayful (i.e., work) behavior (Wiltz & Fein, 2006). Play typically has the following characteristics: it is active (physically and/or mentally); enjoyable (i.e., fun); flexible and changing (elaborated); and focused on the process, not on a product or result. Most important, it is directed by the players. That is, an activity is play only when the players have some internal control (they decide when and what to do), internal motivation (they want to play), and internal reality (they create their own "low risk" worlds) (Bergen, 1987; Neumann, 1971). One child explained how work differs from play in this way: "It's play when you don't have to finish." Many physical, cognitive, language, and social-emotional processes are involved in the play act. Research indicates that play, especially pretense, is related to theory of mind development, problem solving and other cognitive strategies, social and linguistic competence, and development of such academic skills as literacy and mathematics (Bergen, 2002).

Of course, both individual and cultural differences characterize specific play behaviors and types of play. Individual differences include play activity levels, attention qualities, and temperament variations. For example, individuals' play styles may be more or less active, their sustained attention to a type of play may be great or minimal, and their openness to new or varied play experiences may be affected by temperament qualities, such as regularity, stimulus intensity, interest in novelty, and general "playfulness" (Barnett, 1998; Lieberman, 1977). Some children are drawn more to object mastery or social mastery, and this penchant may direct their play activity (Shore, 1998). Children with disabilities may show delays in play development or demonstrate distortions from "typical" play for their age level (Hughes, 1998). Children who have endured severe trauma often play in atypical ways, and there may even be some differences related to gender. Many of the differences in observed play may be culturally influenced, however (Roopnarine, Lasker, Sacks, & Stores, 1998). For example, the types of toys and other play materials provided, the time available for play, and the types of play approved for boys and girls in the culture will influence the expression of play. Other cultural differences may be found in parent play interaction style, in age levels when certain types of play are prominent, and even in the general culture's approval of play as a worthwhile activity.

Even with all of these differences, however, everyone, at some time in their lives, has probably played, and thus has experienced the qualities that make play so valuable. Indeed, play seems to be a "built-in" part of human experience. The big question, therefore, is "why do people play?" Various theorists have addressed this question. For example, Piaget (1962) found play to be the way children organize and make meaning out of their experiences; that is, it is the way they construct knowledge. Vygotsky (1967) agreed about this function of play and also stressed the socialization and self-regulation qualities that play promotes (Bodrova & Leong, 2006). Erikson (1977) focused on the ability of play to increase children's mastery over their social-emotional experiences, and he described how play is the foundation for important rituals followed throughout human life. Biological theory suggests that play serves as the balancer of the "optimal arousal level" that each person seeks (Berlyn, 1969). That is, if the environment is under-stimulating, play is used to make situations more interesting and challenging. Evolutionary theory even more strongly suggests that play has contributed to the survival of the human species by making people more flexible and able to adapt to uncertain conditions in the world (Barnett, 1998; Ellis, 1998).

The majority of these theoretical explanations were made when brain research was still in its infancy; it is only in the last 20 years that scientifically based explorations of internal brain activity have led to theorizing about how brain structures might have a role in play development. Recently, as methods for studying activity in various parts of the brain have emerged, certain sites in the brain are being posited as areas where a "play structure" is located. Thus, play's usefulness in brain development is being hypothesized. For example, Sylwester (1995) has noted that the frontal lobe of the brain has enormous capacity for critical thinking and problem solving, probably in order to make humans prepared for action in response to crises. Sylwester suggests that play may exercise the frontal lobe when there are no survival-related crises to handle, thus keeping that area primed. Much more knowledge about the brain is needed, however, in order to investigate this hypothesis and others that posit play and brain relationships.

What Do We Know About the Brain?

One benefit of recent brain research is that educators can be more enlightened about brain structures and functions, thereby helping them to speculate as to ways brain growth and neurological development are related to play and learning (Bergen & Coscia, 2001). Presently, scientists have a relatively clear picture of the basic components of the nervous system, the structures in the brain, and the role these components and structures play in human physical and mental functioning. To understand how play may be related to the brain, it is necessary to understand how the brain is structured and how it functions. (For further details on brain research, see Bergen & Coscia, 2001.)

Brain Structures

The structures of the brain are made up of nerve cell bodies (soma), fibers (axons and dendrites), glia (supporting and activating cells), and blood vessels. There are also a series of open spaces (ventricles) through which cerebrospinal fluid flows. This fluid serves as a shock absorber and helps maintain the shape of the softer brain tissue. In general, the major anatomical divisions of the brain (hindbrain or brain stem, midbrain, limbic system, forebrain or cerebrum) are successively more complex in organization (Goldberg, 1990). Many animal brains contain structures similar to the hindbrain and midbrain, but their forebrain is not well developed in comparison to that of humans. This diagram of the brain shows its major structures.

Figure 1
Model of the Brain

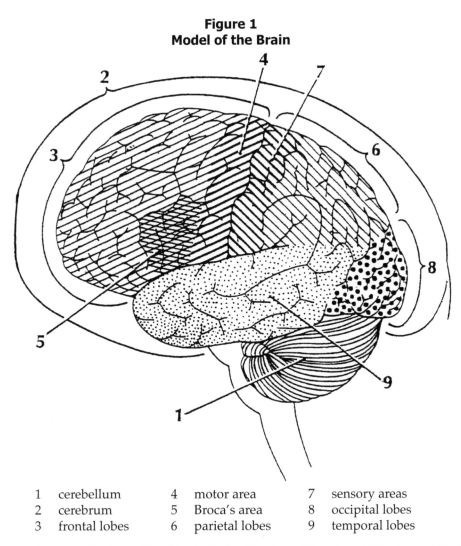

1	cerebellum	4	motor area	7	sensory areas
2	cerebrum	5	Broca's area	8	occipital lobes
3	frontal lobes	6	parietal lobes	9	temporal lobes

Diagram from **Brain Basics,** *published by the National Institute of Neurological Disorders and Stroke.*

In the hindbrain (brain stem), the cerebellum controls balance, posture, motor coordination, and body space awareness. Recent research indicates that the cerebellum also has some involvement with attention, memory, learning, and touch (Lezak, 1995). The medulla regulates such functions as breathing, swallowing, and blood pressure, as well as reflex actions like sneezing. Through the medulla run the afferent (*to* higher processing brain centers) and efferent (*from* higher processing brain centers) fibers or axons that connect receptors and effectors in other parts of the body to the central nervous system (CNS). The pons links the cortex with the cerebellum and has a role in facial expression and eye movement. In the midbrain, a network of interconnected nerve cell bodies and fibers form the reticular formation, which holds the reticular activating system (RAS) responsible for controlling wakefulness and alertness.

Embedded within the cerebral cortex (cerebrum) is the area called the limbic system ("inner brain"). It includes the thalamus, which relays and integrates information from sensory systems to the cortex; the hypothalamus, which is the master controller of the autonomic nervous system; the hippocampus, which is involved in emotional reactions, learning, and memory; and the amygdala, which perceives and interprets emotions and receives olfactory information. The thalamus also plays a role in alerting processing and response systems and

Figure 2
Structures of the Brain: Brain Stem and Limbic System

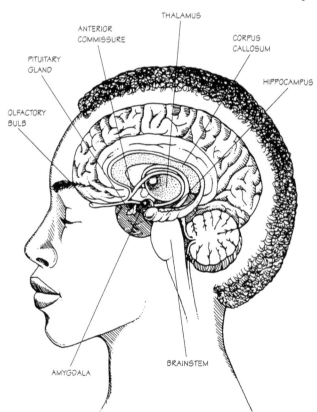

regulating higher level brain activity. The hypothalamus, through its control of the autonomic system, governs heart rate, body temperature, appetite and thirst, and sleep/waking cycles through both sympathetic (increasing physical responses) and parasympathetic (decreasing physical responses) processes. Through the pituitary gland, the hypothalamus also governs the endocrine system, which has glands located throughout the body that secrete hormones necessary for growth, sexual development, and other functions. Recent research suggests that these structures are in close interaction with structures in the cortex, and thus they play a role in higher order thinking as well. The diagram on p. 12 shows one half of the brain, exposing the limbic system.

The cerebrum has two hemispheres (right, left) and four lobes in each hemisphere. Each hemisphere contains white matter (axon, dendrites) and gray matter (cell bodies). The cortex has dense folds that in the adult brain, if stretched flat, would cover about 2.5 square feet. There are four lobes in each hemisphere: frontal, parietal, occipital, and temporal, and each has some distinctive functions. Although specific behaviors are not totally localized in only one part of the brain, the top of the frontal lobe has been identified as the primary motor cortex, and the middle holds an area having primary motor control of language (usually more pronounced in the dominant hemisphere). Located in the front of the cortex (prefrontal lobe) is the primary site of such functions as initiative, drive, ability to control impulses and follow social rules, and ability to perceive and reflect on actions. The somatosensory cortex, which primarily governs sensory processing, is located in the parietal lobe, and this lobe also has an area that controls perception and interpretation of written language. Vision is located primarily in the occipital (back) lobe and hearing and sound localization are in the temporal (side) lobe, which also contains an area identified as vital for the interpretation of spoken language.

Brain Functions

Although some brain areas seem to be primary in carrying out certain functions, there is much integration; that is, many other parts of the brain are involved in these functions. The axons within each hemisphere extend into subcortical areas and traverse the brain midline to connect the two hemispheres through the corpus callosum. While some hemisphere specialization has been identified, there is also much congruence in adult left/right hemisphere responses. Usually, the dominant hemisphere (for most people, this is the left) is slightly larger, while certain areas in the right hemisphere may be larger (e.g., visual-spatial). The frontal lobe shows little anatomic asymmetry, however (Lezak, 1995). The hemispheres' special functions are most evident in the dominance of speech expression and sequential processing in the left hemisphere and in the ability to mediate complex, difficult to verbalize stimuli in the right hemisphere. The left hemisphere also may be superior in processing detailed information, while the right hemisphere may be superior in processing large-scale or global concepts. Researchers have discovered the right hemisphere's capacities for comprehension and seeing relationships, which are necessary for understanding alternative meanings and enjoying jokes (Lezak, 1995). Normal behavior, however, is a function of the whole brain, with both hemispheres contributing to most activities and emotions. Complex mental tasks, such as reading or mathematics and effective storing and retrieving of memories, need the active engagement of both hemispheres.

The communication functions of the brain are carried out by the neurons, each of which is composed of a cell body, one axon (the sending unit), and a number of dendrites (receiving units). Neurons are not attached to each other; rather, there are gaps, called synapses, between the axon and dendrites of each neuron. Each neuron communicates through electrical impulses sent through the axon and dendrites, and through chemical agents (neurotransmitters) that "jump the gap" at the synaptic site. More than 100 neurotransmitters are activated by the correct "fit" with certain receptor sites. Each class of neurotransmitters appears to be involved with particular categories of activation, such as memory or emotional arousal. The brain also contains blood vessels that nourish the neurons, thus enabling them to function.

The messages sent by neurons are communicated among the structures of the brain and also through the spinal cord to and from the nerves in the rest of the body. Together, the brain and spinal cord form the central nervous system (CNS). The supporting glia cells provide a fatty substance (myelin) that coats the axons, making message transmission faster and more efficient. Within the brain, neurons from various structures communicate; those concerned with processing emotions communicate with those involved in rational decision-making, and both communicate with the autonomic system. For example, if the emotional centers of the brain identify that a child is fearful, this emotion may interfere with the child's ability to learn and remember information, and it also may cause such physical stress symptoms as an upset stomach (Perry, 1995). Messages communicated to and from the brain to the body also regulate behavior and thought. For example, the sensory and motor centers of the brain direct the muscles involved in walking; when a person encounters rough pavement, for example, sensory and motor messages from the legs provide information to the brain, signaling the subtle changes in motor coordination that must be made. The basic neuronal communication system is shown in the diagram on p. 15.

Brain Development

At birth, infants have about 100 billion neurons, each of which can produce up to 15,000 synapses when they are well-nourished and adequately stimulated (Lezak, 1995). Synaptogenesis occurs rapidly during the first years; by 12 months, the activity of the brain is more similar to that of the adult brain than the newborn brain. The visual cortex also develops rapidly during this period. The brain's weight increases from about 1 pound at birth to 2 pounds by one year, partly due to the increase in synapses and partly due to the coating of nerve axons with fatty glial cells (myelination), which act to speed neural signals. During the toddler age period, the synapses continue to expand and reach about 1,000 trillion—twice the density of the adult brain. The toddler brain is 2-1/2 times as active as the adult brain and, as the glial cells coat the axons, the weight of the brain continues to increase. Due to the rapid expansion of synapses and the myelination of the axons, a 6-year-old child's brain has reached about 90 percent of its adult weight. When a brain area has amassed many synaptic connections, a pruning process begins, in which synapses that have not been frequently activated start to disappear.

Some synaptic growth continues at later age levels when new information is learned and used, although there appear to be "sensitive periods" for synaptic growth in certain areas of the brain. For example, the visual cortex matures early, so synaptic density is at its greatest during the first years and pruning begins in early childhood. On the other hand, synaptogenesis in the frontal lobe is most prominent during the latter part of early childhood, and pruning in this area begins in earnest in middle and later childhood. From ages 3 to 8, the fastest growth is in the frontal lobe networks, and the speed of processing, memory,

Figure 3
Neuronal Communication System

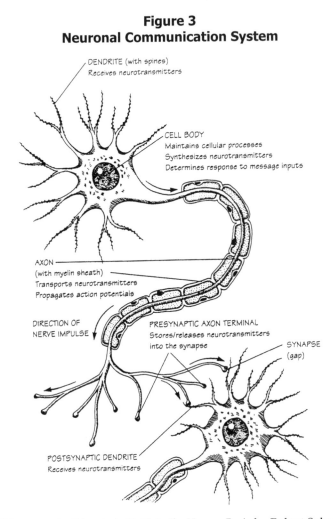

and problem solving are thus increasing. The frontal lobe of the cortex is at its most dense around age 7. During ages 8 through 14, the maturation of the frontal lobe continues and pruning begins in this area. Myelination of these higher brain centers also continues and is completed by late adolescence.

Recent advances in techniques to observe the electrical and chemical processes occurring in living brains have enabled researchers to explain more about how the brain develops. Because 75 percent of brain development occurs after birth, the experiences children have during their early years (and that includes their play experiences!) profoundly affect the ways their individual brains are structured and the ways they perform. By adulthood, each individual's brain is uniquely constructed. While the brain's "plasticity" and resilience provides some protection against early negative experiences, extreme neglect, abuse, starvation, illness, or environmental toxins are likely to cause major long-term damage. Because the brain continues to have some plasticity, experiences throughout life also affect brain structures and functions; thus, people's choices of experiences (as well as their choices of play) continue to affect their brain's development

What Parts of the Brain Are Involved in Play?

Recently, neuropsychological researchers have been speculating on how youthful play may be a major enhancer of brain development. However, the majority of current neuropsychological research connecting play and brain development has focused on non-human animal play. The study of young children's brains is still too intrusive for much direct research.

Animal Play

Animal researchers have noted that the proportionate size of the brain (in relation to an animal's overall size) is related to the amount of playful behavior observed in 15 different orders of mammals (Iwaniuk, Nelson, & Pellis, 2001). That is, the greater the proportion of the body devoted to the brain, the more extensive and long-lasting is play in that order of mammals. The human mammal was not included in this study, but it is likely that the same results would hold true, since humans play more extensively, longer, and in more complex ways than do other playful mammals. In addition, of course, the proportion of overall size taken up by the brain in humans is extremely high in childhood and even in adulthood, in comparison to brain proportions in most animals. Researchers have studied how play is related to brain development in a variety of mammals, including cats, rats, coyotes, and mice (Bekoff & Byers, 1998). For example, Byers and Walker (1995) studied cerebellum development in cats, rats, and mice and found that the motor play of all three species was at its most intense during the peak synaptic growth in the cerebellum, which controls fine motor skills. They indicate that the timing of playful stages in young animals represents important clues to brain development and that the larger brains of some animals are less hard-wired and more sensitive to play influences. In particular, the cortex and cerebellum are parts of the brain that may need play in order to achieve their optimum development.

Siviy (1998) found that rough and tumble play increases the neurochemicals associated with pleasure and excitement in rats, and he suggests that play may activate many parts of the animal brain and stimulate the growth of nerve cells. Other research by Siviy and a colleague (Siviy & Panksepp, 1987) showed that the ability of the thalamus to relay somatic stimuli affects the types of play actions in rough and tumble play but not the animals' play motivation. In another study of rough and tumble play in rats, Gordon, Burke, Akil, Watson, and Panksepp (2003) found that the amygdala and dorsolateral frontal cortex had elevated brain-derived neurotrophic factor (BDNF), which indicates that play may help program higher brain regions involved in emotional behaviors.

In studies of coyote pups, Bekoff (2001) found that coyotes' play seemed to activate many different parts of the brain; he suggests that because of the cognitive involvement in play, animals may have more behavioral flexibility and better learning potential. Different types of play may affect different areas of the brain. According to Lewis (2000), the larger the neocortex is in a species, the more social play they show. Most of these animal researchers stress that being deprived of play may prevent certain brain areas from developing to their fullest potential. Many more studies directly linking play to brain structures and functions are needed before specific information about these links can be claimed. However, research with non-human animals regarding their play behavior is presently an area of increasing study, and the accumulating evidence is pointing to the importance of play in certain sensitive periods of development.

Children's Play

So far, few studies have explored the direct brain links to children's play. One study of testosterone levels in children during free play indicates that a positive relationship exists in boys between testosterone levels and "serious" aggression in social interactions, but there is no similar relationship between testosterone levels and "playful" aggression (Sanchez-Martin et al., 2000). Since the brain triggers the release of hormones, this may be another indication of differences in brain activity during play. Some hypotheses about the importance of play in fostering the development of the frontal lobe in children have been proposed (Panksepp, 1998). Brain imaging studies of children diagnosed with ADHD appear to show delays in the development of frontal lobe areas that are involved in inhibition of action, planning, and conceptualization of complex tasks. Panksepp has hypothesized that these children's active behaviors may be signaling a need for a longer period of rough and tumble play, and that drugs to inhibit ADHD activity may further inhibit the development of their frontal lobes. Another type of evidence for the connection between active play and brain functioning is found in the studies of effects of school recess on children's ability to attend to schoolwork (Pellegrini & Bjorklund, 1996). This research indicates that having an active play period at recess enhances later attention to school tasks.

Although neuroimaging studies have not yet demonstrated the specific neurological connections between play development and brain development in humans, a comparison of these two areas of development certainly suggests that they are related. Given what is known at the present time, it is not possible to reach firm conclusions regarding play's role in brain development. However, brain development does parallel play development in some major ways. As more research is conducted, explanations about the direct linkages between play and the brain will become clearer.

How Does Play Promote Brain Development?

While the actual brain structures that are involved in play have yet to be made explicit, it is possible to compare brain development at various age levels and the play behaviors exhibited at those same age periods in order to hypothesize about play and brain connections (Bergen, 2003).

During the period from birth to age 1, there is a great deal of brain development; this is also the time when play development begins. The connecting process (synaptogenesis) is rapid during this year, with the sensorimotor areas most active during the period of age 2 to 3 months, and the frontal lobe becoming active by 6-8 months. Infants' play during this period follows a pattern that reflects the development of the brain areas that are most active. Much early play involves practice of the sensorimotor system. For example, infants love to observe interesting patterns and colors, explore textures and sounds, grasp objects, and perform various actions on objects. Because of the repetitive nature of their play, Piaget has called it "practice play." When the frontal lobe begins to be activated, the social nature of play expands (with simple turn-taking games like "peek-a-boo" enjoyed), more elaborate practice play with objects occurs, and one-word naming of play objects is common ("baa" for ball).

The period from 2 to 3 years is one of extremely rapid brain development and play development. The structures of the brain that are sensitive to language production (Broca) and comprehension (Weirnicke) become active and language typically develops during this period. Because the areas of the brain that generate social-emotional responses (amygdala/limbic system) begin to be connected with frontal lobe areas, initial understanding of emotions begins, but self-control of emotions is still difficult. Interestingly, by age 2, the first occurrences of pretend play are evident, indicating that the brain is now capable of simple symbolic thought. Children begin to transform actions and objects in play by "feeding" dolls, "driving" trucks, and building "garages." Language is also played with in rhymes and songs and "silly" sounds, and pretend characters can "talk," expressing emotions as well as actions. For example, children can make pretend characters show fear or anger and can interpret that behavior in words ("I'm mad").

During the 3 to 8 years age period, the synaptic connections in motor and sensory areas are firmly established and the process of eliminating synapses (pruning) in these areas has begun. Because of the activity in the higher brain "control" centers, children's levels of attention, and their ability to inhibit impulses, increase. Some evidence indicates that spurts in cortical growth seem to parallel cognitive stage theories. Thus, play during this period is at its most elaborate and extensive. Early pretense has blossomed into sociodramatic play in which children engage in complex theme play, involving roles, scripts, and costumes (for example, "doctor's office," "princesses," or "Superman saving the world"). By age 6, games with rules become a pervasive play activity, and much negotiation of rules, discussion of "fairness," and both cooperation and competition occur in spontaneous and traditional games. Through their play, children demonstrate their extensive symbolic thought capacities and their ability to self-regulate and explain their behavior.

In the 8 to 12 years age period, speed and efficiency of thought increases, spatial working memory improves, emotional regulation becomes greater, planning and problem-solving skills increase, and scientific reasoning and an ability to understand one's own thinking (metacognition) develop. Children still use a larger area of the brain than an adult would use in carrying out discrimination tasks, however. By this age, stable, individual differences in brain structures and functions emerge, and the play of children becomes more sophisticated and individualized. Play also becomes increasingly symbolic, with pretend themes often carrying on for weeks or months (but usually in the privacy of the home). Symbolic games, such as Monopoly and certain computer games, are popular, and the more elaborate the rules, the better. Although some informal games with rules continue, many children are introduced to adult-controlled, highly organized games (e.g., sports), which require greater control of motor, social, and cognitive processes. Children introduced to sports that require more of these abilities than their brains are ready for often experience frustration and lose interest.

The adolescent brain is still developing, with myelination of the frontal lobe continuing; as this occurs, the adolescent is increasingly able to think efficiently, gain further self-regulation, and engage in hypothetical thought. The brain is generally matured by late adolescence, but changes in brain structure and functioning will continue throughout life, as new experiences occur. Although play is a primary activity of the young, playfulness and play activity also continue throughout life. Adolescents play extensively with ideas, and engage in imaginative choices that often involve risk taking. With their friends, they may create their own reality worlds. Constructive play, in which a product is achieved, is also evident in adolescent and adult hobbies. Many social activities also involve play and ritual, pretend schemes (e.g., Klingon language and costumes), and enjoyment of playful sensorimotor activities (e.g., "pick up" games of basketball). Older children and adults engage in many symbolic games (such as Monopoly), sports-related play (such as golf or mountain climbing), and socially acceptable forms of pretense through use of computer-aided virtual realties or actual role-taking in little theater. With maturity, play may still have an important role in keeping the brain active and preventing deterioration of the neuronal networks. Some studies of senior citizens are beginning to show that maintenance of brain functioning also can be enhanced through playful activities and thinking games (e.g., crossword puzzles). The enormous elaboration of adult playful behavior seen in present times is a confirmation of the frontal lobe's need for stimulation when there are no survival crises to engage its full powers.

Summary

At all ages, the developing brain is active and the active brain is the developing brain. Although understanding of the specific ways that play aids brain development awaits more neuropsychological research, the apparent parallels between play development and brain development indicate that enhancing children's play skills and giving many opportunities for play is likely to be useful in helping the brain develop well. At present, there is no research that points to specific play or creative activities, such as listening to Mozart, as being especially useful to the brain. However, many aspects of play are likely to enhance brain development. The most important role that play has is to help children to be physically and mentally active, to have control and choices, to solve problems, and to practice actions to mastery. Until more is known about how specific types of play might enhance particular brain structures or functions, a variety of play experiences in a wide range of content areas is probably warranted to promote the development of a complex and integrated brain.

Play that links sensorimotor, cognitive, and social-emotional experiences together provides an ideal setting for brain development. The play choices children make will not only enhance synaptic growth at an early age but also affect pruning at a later age. Those activities that are most practiced are likely to be the ones that become more stable when pruning is occurring. Thus, play seems important not only for enhancing children's physical development but also for fostering development of cognition, language, social skills, emotional regulation, and creativity. Unfortunately, in the formal education system, play often has been considered an unimportant or even meaningless activity, and it is rarely included in the school curriculum. As brain research begins to give more evidence of the play and brain connection, perhaps play will begin to be more valued by schools. Until then, pursuits of a wide range of play experiences, recreational activities, symbolic games, and creative pretense may help children's brains develop richly and uniquely and keep adult brains active and efficient. Play at all ages seems to have a role in promoting and enriching brain development.

References

Barnett, L. (1998). The adaptive powers of being playful. In S. Reifel (Ed.), *Play and culture studies* (Vol. 1, pp. 97-120). Stamford, CT: Ablex.

Bekoff, M. (2001). Social play behaviour: Cooperation, fairness, trust and the evolution of morality. *Consciousness Studies, 8*, 81.

Bekoff, M., & Byers, J. (Eds.). (1998). *Animal play.* London: Cambridge University Press.

Bergen, D. (Ed.). (1987). *Play as a medium for learning and development.* Portsmouth, NH: Heinemann.

Bergen, D. (2002). The role of pretend play in children's cognitive development. *Early Childhood Research &* *Practice [Online], 4*(1). Available: http//ecrp.uiuc.edu/v4n2/bergen.html

Bergen, D. (2003). *ACEI speaks: Play's role in brain development.* Olney, MD: Association for Childhood Education International.

Bergen, D., & Coscia, J. M. (2001). *Brain research and childhood education: Implications for educators.* Olney, MD: Association for Childhood Education International.

Berlyn, D. E. (1969). Laughter, humor, and play. In G. Lindzey & E. Aronson (Eds.), *The handbook of social psychology* (Vol. 3, pp. 795-852). Reading, MA: Addison-Wesley.

Bodrova, E., & Leong, D. (2006). Adult influences on play: The Vygotskian approach. . In D. P. Fromberg & D. Bergen (Eds.), *Play from birth to twelve: Contexts, perspectives, and meanings* (2nd ed.; pp. 167-172). New York: Routledge.

Byers, J. A. & Walker, C. (1995). Refining the motor training hypothesis for the evolution of play. *American Naturalist, 146*(1), 24-40.

Ellis, M. J. (1998). Play and the origin of the species. In D. Bergen (Ed.), *Readings from play as a medium for learning and development* (pp. 29-31). Olney, MD: Association for Childhood Education International.

Erikson, E. H. (1977). *Toys and reason.* New York: Norton.

Goldberg, S. (1990). *Clinical neuroanatomy made ridiculously simple.* Miami, FL: MedMaster, Inc.

Gordon, N. S., Burke, S., Akil, H., Watson, S. J., & Panksepp, J. (2003). Socially induced brain "fertilization": Play promotes brain derived neurotrophic factor transcription in the amygdala and dorsolateral frontal cortex in juvenile rats. *Neuroscience Letters, 341*(1), 17-20.

Hughes, F. P. (1998). Play in special populations. In O. N. Saracho & B. Spodek (Eds.), *Multiple perspectives on play in early childhood* (pp. 171-193). Albany, NY: State University of New York Press.

Iwaniuk, A. N., Nelson, J. E., & Pellis, S. M. (2001). Do big-brained animals play more? Comparative analyses of play and relative brain size in mammals. *Journal of Comparative Psychology, 115*(1), 29-41.

Lewis, K. (2000). A comparative study of primate play behaviour. *Folla Primatologica,* 71.

Lezak, M. D. (1995). *Neuropsychological assessment* (3rd ed.). New York: Oxford.

Lieberman, J. N. (1977). *Playfulness: Its relationship to imagination and creativity.* New York: Academic Press.

Neumann, E. A. (1971). *The elements of play.* New York: MSS Information Corp.

Panksepp, J. (1998). Attention deficit hyperactivity disorders, psychostimulants, and intolerance of childhood playfulness: A tragedy in the making? *Current Directions in Psychological Science, 7*(3), 91-98).

Pellegrini, A., & Bjorklund, D. F. (1996). The place of recess in school: Issues in the role of recess in children's education and development (Introduc-tion to theme issue, J. Johnson, Theme Coordinator). *Journal of Research in Childhood Education, 11*(1), 5-13.

Perry, B. D. (1995). Incubated in terror: Neurodevelopmental factors in the "cycle of violence." In J. D. Osofsky (Ed.), *Children, youth and violence: Searching for solutions* (pp. 2-20). New York: Guilford.

Piaget, J. (1962). *The origins of intelligence in children.* New York: International Universities Press.

Roopnarine, J. L., Lasker, J., Sacks, M., & Stores, M. (1998). The cultural contexts of children's play. In O. N. Saracho & B. Spodek (Eds.), *Multiple perspectives on play in early childhood* (pp. 194-219). Albany, NY: State University of New York Press.

Sanchez-Martin, J. R., Fano, E., Ahedo, L., Cardas, J., Brain, P. F., & Azpiroz, A. (2000). Relating testosterone levels and free play social behavior in male and female preschool children. *Psychoneuroendocrinology, 25*(8), 773-783.

Shore, C. (1998). Play and language: Individual differences as evidence of development and style. In D. P. Fromberg & D. Bergen (Eds.), *Play from birth to twelve and beyond: Contexts, perspectives, and meanings* (pp. 165-174). New York: Garland Press.

Siviy, S. M. (1998). Neurobiological substrates of play behavior: Glimpses into the structure and function of mammalian playfulness. In M. Bekoff & J. Byers (Eds.), *Animal play: Evolutionary, comparative, and ecological perspectives.* New York: Cambridge University Press.

Siviy, S. M., & Panksepp, J. (1987). Juvenile play in the rat: Thalamic and brain stem involvement. *Physiology & Behavior, 41*(2), 103-114.

Spodek, B., & Saracho, O. (1987). The challenge of educational play. In D. Bergen (Ed.), *Play as a medium for learning and development* (pp. 9-22). Portsmouth, NH: Heinemann.

Sylwester, R. (1995). *A celebration of neurons: An educator's guide to the human brain.* Alexandria, VA: Association for Supervision and Curriculum Development.

Vygotsky, L. (1967). Play and the role of mental development in the child. *Soviet Psychology, 5,* 6-18.

Wiltz, N. W. & Fein, G. G. (2006). Play as children see it. In D. P. Fromberg & D. Bergen (Eds.), *Play from birth to twelve: Contexts, perspectives, and meanings* (2nd ed.; pp. 127-140). New York: Routledge.

Playful Activities as Mediators in a Culturally and Linguistically Diverse World: A Global Perspective

Tunde Szecsi & Debra A. Giambo

For young children, play is a natural activity. Theorists, practitioners, and parents agree that children, regardless of their cultural backgrounds, enthusiastically engage in play. Elkind (2003) states that play is "as fundamental a human disposition as loving and working" (p. 46). To differentiate play activities from non-play behaviors, Isenberg and Quisenberry (2002) characterize play as: 1) intrinsically motivated and self-initiated, 2) process-oriented, 3) non-literal and pleasurable, 4) exploratory and active, and 5) rule-governed. This chapter will examine a sampling of playful activities from around the world, initiated by children, parents, and teachers, to shed light on the unique cultural and linguistic features and benefits of play.

Play is beneficial for children in constructing and refining skills in all developmental domains (Fromberg, 2002). Current brain research suggests that play is a critical initiator of and tool for children's learning (Shore, 1997), as well as a good indicator of the level of brain development (Bergen & Coscia, 2001). In harmony with these findings, studies indicate a strong positive relationship between age-appropriate play and attention, problem solving, memory, and language (Jensen, 2000; Roskos & Neuman, 1998).

The early years are crucial for the development of cultural and linguistic skills. These skills grow during play in which children develop skills, concepts, dispositions about themselves and others, and appropriate social and moral behaviors (Berk, 2002; Bodrova & Leong, 1996). For instance, during play and interactions with others, children as young as age 2 through age 6 construct their identity and develop perceptions about others, including racial awareness (Katz, 1982). Also through play, children can master language skills in their native language as well as acquire an awareness of, and skills in, other languages. However, differences in children's cultural environments may result in varying processes of native and foreign language acquisition (Yule, 2006). Thus, the integration of play, because of its significant influence on development, has become an integral part of the early childhood curriculum in several countries (e.g., the United States, the Netherlands, Hungary, Japan) and an emerging issue in countries traditionally using academic-oriented programs for young children (e.g., China and India) (Roopnarine, Lasker, Sacks, & Stores, 1998).

As a result of increased mobility in our global world, the connections between cultures and linguistic communities have become more common, and teachers find a steadily growing number of culturally and linguistically diverse students in their classrooms. This global dynamic calls for educators to become aware of diverse play patterns across cultures, and thereby create a culturally and linguistically responsive curriculum by which to promote appreciation of cultures and languages at a critical young age. In concordance with this urgent demand, Soto and Negrón (1994) also express the need for studies that investigate children's play behaviors from the perspective of their cultural identities. Thus, the examination of play activities across cultures, as in this chapter, might provide insight into the diverse pathways of how play can effectively facilitate children's cultural and linguistic competencies.

This chapter explores examples of play activities of children, from birth to early adolescence, from cultures outside the United States. The terms "play" and "play activities" are used here in a broad sense to accommodate the diverse definition of play across various cultures. This chapter discusses the following aspects of play as a mediator: 1) operating within a cultural context, 2) conveying the native culture, 3) fostering acceptance of other cultures, 4) facilitating native language development, and 5) transmitting knowledge of other languages. To avoid making generalizations that assume that all children in a given country participate in the same play activities, the term "cultural communities" (Göncü, Mistry, & Mosier, 2000) will be used to indicate communities of people with shared values within a nation.

Cultural Contexts of Play

Despite the universality of play as a natural childhood activity, the contexts of play vary significantly across cultures. Play and its effects on child development can be interpreted in relation to the values and beliefs of the cultural community. The culturally based perception of play seems to have a significant impact on how parents and teachers incorporate play in the school curriculum or at home. Additionally, play varies across cultures, depending on the participants, environments, and resources. These various approaches toward, and opportunities for, play seem to emerge from diverse cultural contexts (Roopnarine et al., 1998).

Perception of Play Across Cultures

Cross-cultural studies of adults' perception of play indicate that play is consciously integrated into the curriculum and the home, but only in cultural communities in which play is considered to be a vital tool for development. Teachers of young children in the Netherlands emphasize the central role of play in development and strive to utilize play-based curricula (Vedder, Bouwer, & Pels, 1996). Similarly, Guatemalan kindergarten teachers seem to advocate for learning through play. Such barriers as large class size and few resources, however, often impede teachers from implementing a play-based curriculum (Cooney, 2004). On the other hand, although teachers in central China appreciate play as an important part of physical development, they assign little importance to play in enhancing intellectual domains (Cooney & Sha, 1999). Furthermore, a comparative study of educational practices in Japan, China, and Korea suggests that in cultures with a more explicit connection with Western educational ideas, such as in Korea, teachers consider play as an invaluable part of curriculum; in China and Japan, however, play does not seem to be perceived as vital for children's development (Ishigaki & Lin, 1999).

Parents' perceptions of their role in play seem to determine the extent to which they participate in play activities. For example, parents in a tribal village in India and in a Mayan peasant community in Guatemala did not view themselves as playmates and demonstrated fewer instances of involvement in play, as compared to parents living in an urban community in Turkey who were more familiar with the educational significance of play (Göncü et al., 2000). Urban Indian parents engaged in play for a different reason. Their purpose was to provide and share enjoyment with their children, rather than offering intellectual stimulation (Roopnarine, Hossain, Gill, & Brophy, 1994). Similarly, in one rural Italian community, mothers considered play as a natural activity. They initiated play for their own pleasure and to enjoy bonding time with their children, rather than for its contributions to cognitive or motor development (New, 1994).

Physical Environment and Resources for Play

The contexts of play are further influenced by the physical environment and the resources available in the cultural communities. Regarding physical environment, Bloch and Adler (1994) observed children in a village in Senegal and noticed that the boys played mainly outside the village, exploring the countryside, while the girls of similar ages generally played in or around the house under the supervision of their mothers. On the other side of the world, the difficult environmental conditions in which the Inuit people live generates children's play activities that primarily focus on survival and hunting skills (Monroe, 1995).

Traditionally, children use materials available in their environment for symbolic play, thereby contributing to the culturally specific features of play. Some examples include children in Japan playing with bamboo horses, children in Taiwan playing chopstick games (Pan, 1994), and girls in Ethiopia using small containers to imitate their mothers getting water from the well (Bloch & Adler, 1994).

As cultures and environments change, the cultural contexts of play and, therefore, the nature of play are constantly changing. For instance, children in Japanese cities, as in many industrialized countries, tend to spend less time outdoors with peers. Consequently, traditional play activities, including hide-and seek, rope-skipping, and spinning tops, tend to disappear, and indoor games, especially involving consumer toys and video games, are becoming more widespread (Takeuchi, 1994).

Play Activities Conveying the Native Culture

Through play, children construct an understanding of the social and cultural norms and customs of their communities. This knowledge is transferred from generation to generation. Therefore, play can be considered an innate medium through which children acquire essential cultural competencies. The culture-specific expectations vary, in part, according to the emphasis on family, group, community, or the individual. Additionally, culturally expected gender roles and gender-based work divisions can be observed in the play-based activities of young children (Fromberg, 2002; Johnson, Christie, & Yawkey, 1999). Hereafter, specific examples for conveying diverse values in collectivist versus individualistic societies, and approaches toward play and work, will be discussed.

Values in Collectivist vs Individualistic Communities

Children learn about culture-specific values and social behaviors through play. Expectations of acculturation in societies differ, according to the manner in which the members of a given society view their roles. From a collectivist point of view, members are expected to be a part of a group, respect group consensus, and avoid conflict; however, from an individualistic point of view, members are understood to be self-centered and self–reliant (Hofstede, 1997). In light of this paradigm, cross-cultural studies highlight the diverse nature of play.

A study of Israeli children's play (Eifermann, 1970) suggests that kibbutz children, raised in a cooperative community, were involved in play activities that required collaboration to achieve a common goal rather than in personal competitive play activities, as it is often seen in individualistic communities. Kibbutz children also were found to prefer games in which members have equal status, unlike games with over- and underprivileged participants.

Similarly, a study of play activities in rural Italy demonstrated how children are prepared to become interdependent members of a group. In mixed-age play groups with little direct adult supervision, the young children in the study negotiated their roles and the rules for such play activities as patty-cake, hide-and-seek, and kickball. Children with such experiences demonstrate from a young age their emerging cultural and linguistic skills, including a sense of membership in the family and the community and competencies about social rules and customs (New, 1994).

Play activities reflecting community expectations also were observed among Marquesan children in Polynesia. The members of this cultural community value group membership; however, they are unwilling to have the will of the other members subsume their personal goals. For example, children as young as 3 seem to avoid play activities with distinctive leaders, elaborate collaboration, and negotiation of rules. This demonstrates how children acquire the modeled and needed social and cultural skills of balancing autonomy and harmony within the group in which they are raised (Martini, 1994).

The Relationship of Play and Labor Within Diverse Cultures

Children develop an emerging understanding about their cultural community's expectations regarding gender roles and gender-specific work in various ways, including play-based observations of adults' work, interactions, and experimentations (Bloch & Adler, 1994; Lancy, 1996). Unlike children in middle-class Euro-American cultures, children in most pre-industrialized communities have daily, direct exposure to adults' work, especially to that of the same-sex parent. There is an expectation that children will learn work-related skills appropriate to their culture for survival purposes. In Kpelle villages in Sierra Leone, learning such gender-specific, work-related skills occurs through make-believe play (Lancy, 1996). For example, young boys engage in hunting play and gradually transition from play to actual hunting. In addition, Bloch (1989) describes Senegalese children's play patterns as "playing at learning the tasks for which they would soon take full responsibility" (p. 139). The divergence between Senegalese boys' and girls' pretend play, including boys herding animals and girls carrying small dolls on their backs, illustrates the ways they learn about their culture-specific gender roles (Bloch & Adler, 1994).

Play Activities Conveying Other Cultures

Children often are exposed to the values, beliefs, and customs of more than one culture. Play, in addition to providing natural trans-cultural experiences, can be an effective mediator of cross-cultural understanding (Derman-Sparks & the A.B.C. Task Force, 1989; Fromberg, 1995). However, research publications addressing the role of child play in conveying the native culture in communities outside the United States far outnumber those related to conveying multicultural awareness through play. This might be indicative of a newer field of research, or of the priority generally given to the native culture. In what follows, examples of culturally specific objects/toys and play activities will provide a glimpse into play patterns that facilitate children's cultural sensitivity to other cultures.

Culturally Specific Objects in the Play Area

Because they have children from diverse cultural backgrounds in their care, including children from Turkey, Suriname, and the Moluccas Islands, child care teachers in the Netherlands created a culturally responsive physical environment with culturally specific toys and objects. For symbolic play, children use a small wooden mosque, a Turkish rug depicting a mosque, cardboard dolls dressed in clothes representing different cultures, Indonesian wayang puppets, dolls with a variety of skin tones, and Turkish shoes and caps. Teachers believe that exposing children to culturally specific play objects helps them make a stress-free contact with other cultures (Vedder et al., 1996).

Culturally Responsive Play Activities

Culturally oriented play activities, including sociodramatic play, games, children's stories, and songs accompanied with dramatization, can help prevent biases and prejudices, and promote positive feelings and behaviors about other cultures (Derman-Sparks & the A.B.C. Task Force, 1989). To help Hungarian children develop understanding and appreciation of the Roma (Gypsy) people, the largest minority in Hungary, teachers often incorporate Roma children's stories, rhymes, and songs with dramatization into the curriculum. Through these play activities, Hungarian children become familiar with Roma values, such as strong family ties, respect for nature, and appreciation of dance and music (Szecsi, 2003). To explore traditions, values, and norms in diverse cultures, children learning foreign languages in Hungarian schools are often involved in play activities incorporating traditional folk games and activities, including making jack-o'-lanterns, dressing up for Halloween, and playing ring games (Szecsi, 2000).

Teachers can utilize play activities to help young children reconsider any inappropriate behaviors toward cultural minorities. For example, a Guatemalan teacher participating in an inservice workshop wrote a puppet play about children who discriminated against and teased a Chinese child (Cooney, 2004). According to Cooney (2004), after subsequent efforts to address cultural conflicts in the classroom, children may become more aware of the feelings associated with being teased and rejected.

Play Activities Facilitating Native Language Development

Children in many cultures engage in play activities that transmit linguistic knowledge about their native language. Some of these activities are taught and passed on among children themselves within communities; others typically occur under the direction of adults, or with adults setting the stage for such play (Fromberg, 1995). Hereafter, we will discuss culture-specific play activities, including sociodramatic play and playful interactions that enhance native language development.

Playful Interactions

The nature and contexts of playful interactions that promote native language development vary across cultures. These interactions, often initiated and maintained by adults, can occur within both the school and the home settings.

The rhymes and tongue twisters commonly enjoyed by children, among other interactions, provide opportunities to learn the native language. For example, in the Dominican Republic, a commonly known rhyme chanted by children during play, "A, e, i, o, u. El burro sabe mas que tu" (A, e, i, o, u. *The burro knows more than you*), helps children learn about vowels. An example of a Dominican tongue twister that makes children aware of consonant blends, in this case, /cr/ and /tr/, is, "En un jardín crepín hau un pontriquito crepín que encrepa la cola y encrepa la crín, ven y empotrate aquí potriquín crepín (*In a garden, there is a wild pony that ruffles his tail and ruffles his mane. Come stand still here, wild pony* (personal communication, B. Fernandez, November 8, 2004). (For more examples, see Garrido de Boggs, 1980.) Similarly, tongue twisters serve as popular, playful interactions between adults and children in Hungary. They focus on sounds difficult to pronounce for young children. The following tongue twister focuses on the rolling /r/ sound that children usually master by age 5: "Répa, retek, mogyoró, korán reggel ritkán rikkant a rigó" (*Carrot, radish, and hazelnuts; in the early morning, the blackbird is rarely calling*).

Children in a rural Italian community demonstrate high levels of verbal negotiation during play. Adults are highly responsive to children and initiate teasing, cajoling, and other verbal interactions with children. These playful conversations are lively, involving multiple partners and reflecting the hierarchy of the cultural community. New (1994) suggests that these rich oral language situations contribute to children's linguistic development, and are embedded in culturally accepted social behaviors.

Learning communication patterns as well as culturally appropriate behaviors occurs during a traditional Korean game known as Yut-Noli. On certain national holidays, such as Chusuk and Korean Thanksgiving Day, families and neighbors play this board game. The game initiates verbal interactions, thus providing a means for children to participate in game-related conversations with adults as well as an opporunity to learn about traditional Korean customs (personal communication, Y. Park, October, 22, 2004).

Sociodramatic Play

Sociodramatic play has the potential to provide children with opportunities to extend their language (Anim-Addo, 1992) and requires the understanding and use of narrative elements, such as characters, plot, sequence, and setting. Children often behave at a level above their developmental age during sociodramatic play, creating the potential for a zone of proximal development and, thus, opportunities for more advanced language use (Forman & McPhail, 1993; Vygotsky, 1978).

Native language growth resulting from sociodramatic play experiences has been documented. In a study of the sociodramatic play of Mexican American pre-kindergartners, children demonstrated a richness of oral language, including the ability to use language, order events sequentially, use story structure (such as beginning, middle, and end), understand story elements (e.g., characters, setting, and plot), report on past/present events, reason, predict, imagine, negotiate, come to agreement, use descriptive language, and understand cause/effect relationships (Riojas-Cortez, 2000). Furthermore, children in Guyana who engaged in regularly scheduled, dramatic, fantasy play demonstrated greater gains in language scores related to mean length of utterance, compared with a control group (Taharally, 1991).

Sociodramatic play often is initiated through sharing folk stories. These stories convey important aspects of the culture to young children, and promote active involvement as well as language enrichment. In addition, dramatized childhood stories teach culture-specific ways of speaking, as well as values and beliefs (Meek, 1991). From birth, Hungarian children are immersed in folktales. The storylines are rich in historical and cultural customs and traditions, exposing children to sophisticated vocabulary and language structures essential during their school years. In addition to listening to folktales, children are involved in related play opportunities. For example, after reading the story *Musicians of Bremen*, preschool children were invited to brainstorm about the outlaws occupying the musicians' home. Upon verbally reaching a consensus about a solution, the children acted out the scene while using appropriate language (Szecsi, 2000).

Play Activities Transmitting Knowledge of Other Languages

Play activities can go beyond the native language and convey knowledge of another language. Therefore, in early foreign or second language learning experiences, we recommend incorporating play into the children's daily program. Here, we present examples of play-based activities in which children were exposed to a foreign or second language.

A study of South Korean children learning English showed that the children participated in interactive role-playing of stories over a four-month period. The results indicated that the children demonstrated significant growth in their English language development, including the number of times they spoke, the number of words they used, and the way in which they managed their communication (Kim & Hall, 2002). Additionally, in English as a second language classes, play helped older Canadian elementary schoolchildren with their ability to communicate and socialize, as well as their sense of independence and self-esteem (Silver, 1999).

In the Russian preschool called Magic World, children ages 3 to 7 with diverse language backgrounds participate in playful activities "to plan their work, find extraordinary ways of solving the problem, and improve the acquired practical skills" (personal communication, M. Sokolaja, October 30, 2004). Playful activities initiated in Russian, which is a second language for most of the children, are accompanied by music and visuals. In this way, teachers arouse children's interest and their motivation to participate in, and build their comprehension of the second language.

In the Maci preschool in Hungary, playful activities, such as large-motor play activities, carving pumpkins, playing Bingo, singing English songs with movement, and dramatizing children's stories, are conducted in English as a foreign language. The children learn the correct pronunciation of English words while playing these games. Teachers also engage children in using puppets to playfully master difficult English sounds that do not exist in Hungarian (Szecsi, 2000). A study (Nikolov, 1995) indicates that young Hungarian children acknowledged playful activities, riddles, and games as reasons for their enjoyment of foreign language classes.

Concluding Thoughts

This chapter provides a glimpse into the unlimited variety and diversity of play activities in a sampling of cultural communities outside the United States. The selected examples focusing on play as a medium for the development of cultural and linguistic awareness indicate the culture-specific nature of play. In cultural communities around the world, play seems to be a fundamental means for becoming familiar with culture and language. However, these play-based experiences greatly vary in terms of the circumstances of play, including participants, locations, and resources, and in terms of the content and competencies related to culture and language.

With the increasing need to create a culturally responsive curriculum, especially for young children, it is becoming more important for educators to become aware of the culture-specific nature of play activities. Such activities can serve as mediators in our culturally and linguistically diverse world. These international examples for enhancing children's cultural sensitivity and promoting first- and second-language learning can offer the added benefit of helping children to feel included and appreciated in their new classroom. In these ways, all children in the classroom can benefit—not only those who are native, but also those new to the culture and language of the school. Thus, when teachers of diverse children enrich their curriculum with play activities used in different cultural communities, the advantages can be far-reaching.

References

Anim-Addo, J. (1992). Drama with young learners in school. In P. Pinsent (Ed.), *Language, culture, and young children* (pp. 70-79). London: David Fulton Publishers.

Bergen, G., & Coscia, J. (2001). *Brain research and childhood education*. Olney, MD: Association for Childhood Education International.

Berk, L. (2002). *Infants, children, and adolescents* (4th ed.). Boston: Allyn & Bacon.

Bloch, M. (1989). Young boys' and girls' play at home and in the community: A cultural-ecological framework. In M. Bloch & A. Pellegrine (Eds.), *The ecological context of children's play* (pp. 120-154). Norwood, NJ: Ablex.

Bloch, M., & Adler, S. (1994). African children's play and emergence of the sexual division of labor. In J. Roopnarine, J. Johnson, & F. Hooper (Eds.), *Children's play in diverse cultures* (pp. 148-178). Albany, NY: State University of New York Press.

Bodrova, E., & Leong, D. (1996). *Tools of mind: The Vygotskian approach to early childhood education*. Englewood Cliffs, NJ: Prentice-Hall.

Cooney, M. (2004). Is play important? Guatemalan kindergartners' classroom experiences and their parents' and teachers' perceptions of learning through play. *Journal of Research in Childhood Education, 18*(4), 261-277.

Cooney, M., & Sha, J. (1999). Play in the day of Qiaoqiao: A Chinese perspective. *Child Study Journal, 29*(2), 97-111.

Derman-Sparks, L., & the A.B.C. Task Force. (1989). *Anti-bias curriculum: Tools for empowering young children*. Washington, DC: National Association for the Education of Young Children.

Eifermann, R. (1970). Cooperativeness and egalitarianism in kibbutz children's games. *Human Relations, 23,* 579-587.

Elkind, D. (2003). Thanks for the memory: The lasting value of true play. *Young Children, 58*(3), 46-52.

Forman, E., & McPhail, J. (1993). Vygotskian perspective on children's collaborative problem-solving activities. In E. Forman, N. Minick, & C. A. Stone (Eds.), *Contexts for learning* (pp. 213-229). New York: Oxford University Press.

Fromberg, D. (1995). Politics, pretend play, and pedagogy in early childhood preservice and inservice education. In E. Klugman (Ed.), *Play, policy, and practice* (pp. 55-69). St. Paul, MN: Readleaf Press.

Fromberg, D. (2002). *Play and meaning in early childhood education*. Boston: Allyn & Bacon.

Garrido de Boggs, E. (1980). *Folklore infantile de Santo Domingo*. Santo Domingo, Dominican Republic: Editora de Santo Domingo.

Göncü, A., Mistry, J., & Mosier, C. (2000). Cultural variations in the play of toddlers. *International Journal of Behavioral Development, 24*(3), 321-329.

Hofstede, G. (1997). *Culture and organizations: Software of the mind*. New York: McGraw-Hill.

Isenberg, J. P., & Quisenberry, N. (2002). Play: Essential for all children: A position paper of the Association for Childhood Education International. *Childhood Education, 79,* 33-39.

Ishigaki, E., & Lin, J. (1999). A comparative study of preschool teachers' attitudes: Towards children's right to play in Japan, China and Korea. *International Journal of Early Childhood, 31*(1), 40-48.

Jensen, E. (2000). Moving with the brain in mind. *Educational Leadership, 58*(3), 34-37.

Johnson, J., Christie, J., & Yawkey, T. (1999). *Play and early childhood development*. New York: Longman.

Katz, P. (1982). Development of children's racial awareness and intergroup attitudes. In L. G. Katz (Ed.), *Current topics in early childhood education* (Vol. 4, pp. 17-54). Norwood, NJ: Ablex.

Kim, D., & Hall, J. K. (2002). The role of an interactive book reading program in the development of second language pragmatic competence. *The Modern Language Journal, 86*(3), 332-348.

Lancy, D. (1996). *Playing on the mother-ground: Cultural routines for children's development*. New York: The Guilford Press.

Martini, M. (1994). Peer interactions in Polynesia: A view from the Marquesas. In J. Roopnarine, J. Johnson, & F. Hooper (Eds.), *Children's play in diverse cultures* (pp. 73-103). Albany, NY: State University of New York Press.

Meek, M. (1991). *On being literate*. London: Bodley Head.

Monroe, J. (1995). Developing cultural awareness through play. *Journal of Physical Education, Recreation & Dance, 66*(8), 24-27.

New, R. (1994). Child's play—una cosa naturale: An

Italian perspective. In J. Roopnarine, J. Johnson, & F. Hooper (Eds.), *Children's play in diverse cultures* (pp. 123-147). Albany, NY: State University of New York Press.

Nikolov, M. (1995). Altalanos iskolas gyerekek motivacioja az angol mint idegen nyelv tanulasara. [Motivation of students in elementary education toward English as a foreign language.] *Magyar Nyelvoktatas, 1*(1), 7-21.

Pan, W. H. L. (1994). Children's play in Taiwan. In J. Roopnarine, J. Johnson, & F. Hooper (Eds.), *Children's play in diverse culture* (pp. 31-50). Albany, NY: State University of New York Press.

Riojas-Cortez, M. (2000). Mexican American preschoolers create stories: Sociodramatic play in a dual language classroom. *Bilingual Research Journal, 24*(3). Retrieved October 28, 2004, from www.brj.asu.edu/v243/articles/art6.html.

Roopnarine, J., Hossain, Z., Gill, P., & Brophy, H. (1994). Play in the East Indian context. In J. Roopnarine, J. Johnson, & F. Hooper (Eds.), *Children's play in diverse culture* (pp. 9-30). Albany, NY: State University of New York Press.

Roopnarine, J., Lasker, J., Sacks, M., & Stores, M. (1998). The cultural context of children play. In O. N. Saracho & B. Spodek (Eds.), *Multiple perspectives on play in early childhood education* (pp. 194-219). Albany, NY: State University of New York Press.

Roskos, K., & Neuman, S. (1998). Play as an opportunity for literacy. In O. N. Saracho & B. Spodek (Eds.), *Multiple perspectives on play in early childhood education* (pp. 100-116). Albany, NY: State University of New York Press.

Shore, R. (1997). *Rethinking the brain: New insights into early development.* New York: Family and Work Institute.

Silver, A. (1999). Play: A fundamental equalizer for ESL children. *TESL Canada Journal, 16*(2), 62-69.

Soto, L. D., & Negrón, L. (1994). Mainland Puerto Rican children. In J. Roopnarine, J. Johnson, & F. Hooper (Eds.), *Children's play in diverse cultures* (pp. 104-122). Albany, NY: State University of New York Press.

Szecsi, T. (2000). *A comparative analysis of two preschools from the perspective of multicultural education.* Unpublished master's thesis. University of Pecs, Pecs, Hungary.

Szecsi, T. (2003). Administrator, teacher educator, mentor teacher and preservice teacher beliefs about diversity in Hungary. *Dissertation Abstracts International, 64*(05), 1609A. (AAT 3089176)

Taharally, L. C. (1991). Fantasy play, language, and cognitive ability of four-year-old children in Guyana, South America. *Child Study Journal, 21*, 37-56.

Takeuchi, M. (1994). Children's play in Japan. In J. Roopnarine, J. Johnson, & F. Hooper (Eds.), *Children's play in diverse culture* (pp. 51-72). Albany, NY: State University of New York Press.

Vedder, P., Bouwer, E., & Pels, T. (1996). *Multicultural child care.* Cleveland, OH: Multicultural Matters Ltd.

Vygotsky, L. S. (1978). *Mind in society.* Cambridge, MA: Harvard University Press.

Yule, G. (2006). *The study of language* (3rd ed.). Cambridge: Cambridge University Press.

The Value and Contribution of Play to Preschoolers' Development

Ernest Dettore, Jr.

Chapter 3

But if society's actions were based on knowledge and research findings alone, then play would be protected and cherished in the homes, neighborhoods, and communities.

—Seefeldt, 1995

"It's the year 2025. A group is embarking on an excursion with all of the markings of an archeological dig. They enter gradually, but with determination, through a sealed passageway to rediscover a long abandoned practice, involving engagement with artifacts only found now in history books or paintings. What this handful of adventurous children and adults are entering is the lost world of play. The artifacts of which I speak are blocks, sand, clay, and dress-up clothes." (Dettore, 2004)

While the above scenario may present an overly bleak view of the future of young children's play, there is evidence that imaginative, child-powered play is disappearing. In a recent report, the Alliance for Childhood (2004) identifies several reasons for the decline of play: 1) increased demand for 3- to 6-year-olds to sit still for academic lessons and standardized testing; 2) children spending too many sedentary hours—often alone—looking at televisions, computers, and video games, which present prepackaged scripts that stunt imagination; 3) loss of time for school recess and of safe green spaces where children can freely explore nature; 4) rushed and overscheduled lives, full of adult-organized or adult-oriented activities; and 5) a glut of toys that take control of play away from children and channel them into violent behavior modeled on popular television, movie, and video game characters. Add to this mix society's renewed emphasis on work rather than play (Seefeldt, 1995), and we begin to understand the underlying principles behind the challenges to play and the activities arbitrarily replacing play.

The paucity of play at home, in neighborhoods, and in schools, and the subsequent undesirable outcomes, have been cited as a great cause for concern by numerous experts in the field of child development, by organizations serving the field of early childhood education, and by organizations advocating for the physical and mental health of children (American Academy of Pediatrics [AAP], 2006; Association for Childhood Education International [ACEI]/Isenberg & Quisenberry, 2002; Seefeldt, 1995; Sutton-Smith, 1988; Zigler et al., 2004).

In its position statement titled *Play: Essential for All Children* (ACEI/Isenberg & Quisenberry, 2002), the Association for Childhood Education International makes clear that "children are growing up in a rapidly changing world characterized by dramatic shifts in what all children are expected to know and be able to do" (p. 1). Throughout history, psychological and educational theorists have believed that play serves a central purpose in the lives of children (Seefeldt, 1995). "Every early childhood theorist of this century has respected the need of young children for play, whether solitary or social" (Sutton-Smith, 1988, p. 298). Yet, "despite decades of research documenting how play has a crucial role in the optimal growth, learning, and development of children from infancy through adolescence, the need for play is being challenged" (ACEI/Isenberg & Quisenberry, 2002, p. 1).

How Is Play Being Challenged?

Experts in the field of early child development, anthropology, psychology, and mental health who are concerned by the loss or severe curtailment of play say that this reduction could affect children's thinking processes, physical well-being, and mental health (Almon, 2003; Furlow, 2001; Levin, 2000; Marcon, 2002; Montague, 1983; Olfman, 2003; Pellegrini & Glickman, 1989; Singer & Singer, 2003; Sutton-Smith, 1988; Wilson, 1998). Joan Almon (2003), President of the Alliance for Children, posits that creative play is a central activity in the lives of healthy children. She cites well-documented research supporting creative play as a staple in children's healthy development. Almon further points out that children's play, in the creative, open-ended sense, is now seriously endangered and explains how the demise of play will certainly have serious consequences for children and for the future of childhood itself.

Sharna Olfman (2003), a developmental and clinical psychologist at Point Park University in Pittsburgh, decries the steady emergence of developmentally inappropriate early childhood education (which is, for example, insensitive to individual learning styles). Such practices have led to an unprecedented increase in the number of young children being labeled and treated for varying degrees of psychiatric illnesses, learning disabilities, and attention disorders. Anthropologist Ashley Montague (1983) explains that "the ability to play is one of the principal criteria of mental health" (pp. 156-157). Bryant Furlow (2001), writing in *New Scientist*, said: "Children destined to suffer mental illnesses such as schizophrenia as adults, for example, engage in precious little social play early in life" (p. 28). It is not yet known whether children who do not play when young are more prone to becoming mentally ill, but there is deep concern in the mental health community that this may be the case.

Longitudinal research by Marcon (2002) supports the value of the child-initiated model of preschool for children from low-income families over programs that emphasize academics and teach particular skills. She concluded that children, especially boys, who were enrolled in preschools emphasizing child-initiated activities demonstrated greater mastery of basic skills than did children in programs emphasizing academics. Furthermore, early learning experiences that emphasized socio-emotional development over academic preparation actually enhanced later academic achievement.

Levin (2000) asserts that "the social and emotional well-being that comes from supporting the development of the whole child is an essential element of effective academic learning. When we fail to support all aspects of children's development, academic achievement suffers." Singer et al. (cited in Olfman, 2003, p. 44) write: "Children who have developed a rich capacity for imaginative play are not only emotionally and socially advantaged, but they are intellectually advantaged as well." Indeed, decades of compelling research has documented that imaginative play is an essential building block for the academic challenges awaiting the preschool child. And yet, as concern about school readiness mounts, a common but misguided response is to sideline play and introduce formal academic lessons to preschool-age children, a trend that is promoted by current federal guidelines in the United States for preschool readiness skills. According to Pellegrini and Glickman (1989), "Recess is one of the few times during the school day when children are free to exhibit a wide range of social competencies—sharing, cooperation, negative and passive language—in the context that they see meaningful" (p. 24). Sluckin (1981) and Sutton-Smith (1971) have long considered social skills learned and practiced on the playground during recess as important to later development. Groos (1909), Piaget (1932), Vygotsky (1978), and Sluckin (1981) all viewed children's play as practice and preparation for adulthood. Neurologist Frank Wilson (1999), who has researched

the relationship of the hand and brain in learning, is deeply concerned that current education trends ignore this relationship. He writes: "I would argue that any theory of human intelligence which ignores the interdependence of hand and brain function . . . is grossly misleading and sterile" (p. 1). Yet, recess opportunities, which facilitate all such development, are being curtailed or cut altogether in far too many schools.

A new report from the American Academy of Pediatrics (2006), titled "The Importance of Play in Promoting Healthy Child Development and Maintaining Strong Parent-Child Bonds," found that free and unstructured play is healthy and, in fact, essential for helping children reach important social, emotional, and cognitive developmental milestones, as well as helping them manage stress and become resilient. Since the challenges to play align with the reasons for its disappearance, a closer look at the Alliance for Childhood's report (2004) on the effects of educational and societal trends on play and the reasons for its marginalization is warranted.

What Are the Effects of Educational Trends Marginalizing Play?

Decline of Play Reason 1: Increased demand for 3- to 6-year-olds to sit still for academic lessons and standardized testing. Psychologist Ed Zigler et al. (2004) cite the No Child Left Behind Act (NCLB) as the latest movement to severely curtail activities that foster social and emotional learning. With NCLB's emphases on a cognitive approach to learning, on academic achievement, and on standardized testing, no time remains for those activities so necessary in early childhood, namely sociodramatic play; hands-on, experiential activities; art; and music. Almon (2003) states that many schools have adopted such strategies as scripted teaching, computerized learning, standardized assessment, and reduced physical education and recess opportunities. These approaches to education actually undermine children's natural opportunities for meaningful and focused life lessons through creative play and may result in children becoming alienated from their school experiences. Educational trends that marginalize play include:

- Higher and tougher standards of learning
- A stronger focus on academic achievement at younger and younger age levels
- State legislatures prescribing kindergarten curricula
- First-grade curriculum being introduced in kindergarten
- The inclusion of scope and sequence charts in kindergarten
- Drill and practice of basic skills replacing exploration and self-discovery
- An increase in academic testing as schools respond to the calls for accountability
- Teachers are under pressure to be accountable and are changing their teaching styles to a back-to-basics style with pencil-and-paper tests
- Schools are eliminating recess
- Difficulty in finding space and materials for play in public schools
- Preschool teachers feeling compelled to prepare children academically for kindergarten
- Preschoolers' focus taken away from play and placed on early reading.

Increasingly, kindergarten has become a full day of school, with nearly the entire time devoted to academic instruction. Children may get 25 minutes of recess, but many teachers report they have no time for indoor socio-dramatic play, despite the abundance of research showing the gains linked to such play for children's overall development. Most disturbing are reports from teachers that when they do give 5-year-olds time to play, the children literally do not know what to do. They have no ideas of their own for how to play.

When children do have time to play, they too often play with a pre-programmed electronic toy or sit in front of a screen—television, computer, or hand-held game—where they respond to a scenario created by someone else. As a result, children are developing a "problem-solving deficit disorder," says Diane Levin (cited in MacPherson, 2004, p. 1), a child development expert at Wheelock College in Boston. Levin further adds that "developing imagination and creativity is essential for children to develop problem-solving skills" (p. 1).

What Are the Effects of Societal Trends Marginalizing Play?

Decline of Play Reason 2: Children spend too many sedentary hours—often alone—looking at televisions, computers, and video games, which present prepackaged scripts that stunt imagination. The American Academy of Pediatrics (Kids Health, 2005) reported an increase in children's activities around televisions, computers, and hand-held video screens. Most children plug into the world of television long before they enter school: 70 percent of child care centers use television during a typical day. In the United States, children watch about 4 hours of television a day—even though the AAP guidelines say children older than 2 should watch no more than 1 to 2 hours a day of quality programming (AAP, 1999). In a year, the average child spends 900 hours in school and nearly 1,023 hours in front of a television (Kids Health, 2005).

The AAP (1999) further asserts that during the first two years, a critical time for children's brain development, television watching can get in the way of exploring, learning, and spending time interacting and playing with parents and others. These activities help young children develop the skills they need to grow cognitively, physically, socially, and emotionally.

Likewise, the Canadian Paediatric Society, in a position statement on the impact of media use on children and youth (2003), reports that children are deprived or short-changed from the benefits of play when involved with screens. Specifically, the potential negative influences from excessive television watching and computer use include:

- An increase in children's violent behavior
- Increased incidence of childhood obesity
- A deleterious effect on learning and academic performance
- Overexposure to commercial products through advertising
- Exposure to violence, inappropriate sexuality, and offensive language from some television programs
- A negative effect on a child's postural development
- Undeveloped social skills
- Some children with seizure disorders are more prone to attacks brought on by a flickering television or computer screen (although this happens rarely).

Decline of Play Reason 3: The loss of time for school recess and of safe green spaces where children can freely explore nature. Dramstad (1999) reports that educators attribute the decline in time set aside for school recess to an upsurge in anxiety about liability if children are injured, concerns about potential danger from child predators, a shortage of teachers and volunteers to supervise children, and the need to dedicate as much of the school day as possible to learning. Administrators, in particular, are under pressure from a number of sources to improve achievement, increase test scores, and make time for other disciplines, such as drama, music, and art (although many schools have dropped those classes as well)—all within a six-hour school day. Condren (2005) credits the shortage of playgounds and green space to the increased litigiousness of society and to property development.

According to Pellegrini and Glickman (1989), recess is one of the few times during the school day when children are free to exhibit a wide range of social competencies—sharing, cooperation, negative and passive language—in the context that they see meaningful. At recess, however, the playground can become one of the few places where children actually define and enforce meaningful social interaction. Without recess, children lose an important educational experience. These social experiences become quite educational:

First, they help the children learn to cooperate to the extent that the play requires cooperation. Second, children learn to solve problems in such forms of play. They realize that in order to sustain their chase play with peers they must take turns being the chaser or the chased. If they refuse to change roles, play ends. The reciprocating role in this type of play is a powerful predictor of the ability to cooperate and view events from different perspectives. (p. 24)

This valuable educational experience is lost to those who do not have recess opportunities. Self (1996) asserts that being outside, including on playgrounds, provides opportunities for children to actively expand and create play environments.

Decline of Play Reason 4: Rushed and overscheduled lives, full of adult-organized or adult-oriented activities. Child development specialist David Elkind (2001) reports that parents are under more pressure than ever to overschedule their children's lives and have them engage in organized sports and other activities that may be age-inappropriate. Most agree that the practice has become a status symbol among families. In short, a superkid is a child pressured by parents and by society in general to do too much, too soon. It's an escalating phenomenon in some societies—with no end in sight. Johann Christoph Arnold (2001) notes that the pressure to excel is undermining childhood as never before. Society is bent on molding children into successful adults, instead of treasuring their genuineness and carefree innocence.

The Illinois Early Learning Project (2004) reports that some doctors and psychologists think that free play and family activities—hiking or playing catch, for example—are healthier for a young child than organized sports activities. Enrolling children in too many activities also may cause unnecessary stress and frustration if children don't share their parents' goals. Many professionals believe that a number of children are too busy in sports, lessons, and clubs and consequently do not have time to play creatively or relax after school. Childhood is not a dress rehearsal for adulthood! It is a separate, unique, and very special phase of life. We are essentially wiping it out of existence in an effort to be sure that our children get ahead (Pica, 2004).

Decline of Play Reason 5: The glut of toys that take control of play away from children and channel them into violent behavior modeled on popular television, movie, and video game characters. Since the Federal Communications Commission deregulated children's television programming in 1984, it has been legal to advertise toys through television programs. As a result, most best-selling toys are linked to children's television shows and other electronic media. Many of these promote violence, focus on sexual behavior and appearance, and encourage buying more and more toys and characters. Deregulation has made choosing toys and creating a healthy play environment more difficult for adults. Many of these action toys cause children to reenact undesirable, violent scripts they have seen on television or in videos. These reenactments often override children's own creative ideas. Two national children's advocacy organizations, TRUCE (Teachers Resisting Unhealthy Children's Entertainment) and the Alliance for Childhood (2004), issued a joint statement warning about "killjoy toys"—products sold as toys that inhibit rather than promote imaginative, creative play. They caution that because of these products, "child-powered" play is endangered.

Joan Almon (2003) of the Alliance for Childhood reports that teachers found children to be increasingly unable to generate their own ideas for play—a critical factor in healthy development. Many high-tech and media-linked toys are highly structured, provide their own scripts, and take control of play away from children. Some children have actually forgotten how to play, or they find playing on their own—minus screens and battery-powered gadgets—too boring. In other cases, their play is violent or disturbed. Almon further asserts that

real play is child-powered and child-initiated—like social "let's pretend" play and the rough and tumble of outdoor games and adventures in nature. It evolves and changes over time. This is play that children can dive into with zest. It's active, fresh every day, never runs out of batteries, never breaks, and needs no warning labels about graphic visuals or audio. (TRUCE, p. 1)

Finally, the last trend that is jeopardizing young children's play is society's renewed emphasis on work over play. Many adults appear astonished by the concept that children need free time to themselves. Adults often assume that play is a waste of time in light of all that children need to learn in a rapidly changing technological world. Play is generally regarded as something done for enjoyment or pleasure, to unwind or relax. It often has been perceived as something "trivial or fruitless" (Kraus, 1990, p. 27). Work is meaningful and purposeful; play, however, is regarded as something people do in their spare time. As one study points out, parents often criticize early childhood programs as "ineffective learning environments because they have emphasized children's play without articulating the goals for children" (National Association for the Education of Young Children, p. 24). Many educators, however, recognize that the major goal of play is to provide children with experiences. Not every action or form of play needs to be, or should be, goal-oriented. Children should be able to play for play's sake; sadly, few parents seem to recognize this. An appraisal of what can be done to restore the value of play should be examined next.

What Can We Do To Revive and Preserve Play?

The value of true play and fantasy/imagination has been dismissed too often and needs to be re-emphasized in our homes and schools. Children need a place and a method for personal expression. Findings from the recent explosion of research on the brain and learning also delineate the importance of play (Jensen, 2000, 2001; Shore, 1997). We know that active brains make permanent neurological connections critical to learning, whereas inactive

brains do not. Brain research demonstrates that play is a scaffold for development, a vehicle for increasing neural structures, and a means by which all children practice the skills they will need later in life. This research (Bergen, 2002; Christie, 2001; Frost, Wortham, & Reifel, 2001; Shore, 1997) contradicts the view of play as trivial, simple, frivolous, unimportant, and purposeless behavior and challenges us to recognize play for what it is—a behavior that has a powerful influence on learning and that should be taken seriously. Such an attitude shift could increase the level of respect accorded to currently undervalued activities such as recess, physical education, the arts, and rich personal adult/child interactions.

The International Play Association USA (2006) is an organization whose purpose is to protect, preserve, and promote play as a fundamental right for all humans. It recommends that early educators:

- Reduce or eliminate screen time: Children may be bored or anxious at first, unsure of how to entertain themselves. Be prepared by providing simple playthings, good storybooks, and suggestions for make-believe play to inspire their inner creativity.
- Choose simple toys for your children: The child's imagination is the engine of healthy play. Simple toys and natural materials, like wood, boxes, balls, sand and shovels, beeswax, clay, stuffed animals, and generic dolls, invite children to create their own scenes—and then knock them down and start over. Battery-driven gadgets distract them from real play.
- Encourage outdoor adventures: Sticks, mud, water, rocks, wind—even bugs and weeds—make a paradise for play. Reserve time every day, when possible, for outdoor play where children can run, climb, find secret hiding places, and dream up dramas.
- Let your work inspire play: When adults are deeply engaged in work—like cooking, raking, cleaning, or washing the car—their example inspires children to deeply immerse themselves in their play. Avoid interrupting or taking over play, but be available as needed. Let children know their play is important.
- Become an advocate for pro-play policies: Share the evidence about the importance of imaginative play in preschool and kindergarten, and of recess for older children, with other parents, teachers, and school officials. Lobby for safe, well-maintained parks in your community. Start an annual local Play Day. (For how-to tips, see www.ipausa.org/playdayorg.htm.)

The Alliance for Childhood promotes policies and practices that support children's healthy development, love of learning, and joy in living. The Alliance is committed to restoring play for children of all ages (and adults, too). It also emphasizes returning play to preschool and kindergarten education, in the interests of fostering physical and social development, language development, imagination, and creative thinking, and enhancing all forms of learning.

The Alliance's Restoring Play Project involves a multi-pronged approach:

- A campaign to restore creative play and hands-on learning in kindergarten and preschool education
- A focus on "playwork" to help adults learn how to support children's play on school playgrounds and in parks, children's museums, and other out-of-school environments
- Research on the current status of play and academic instruction in preschools and kindergartens
- Support for public education efforts in conjunction with the forthcoming PBS documentary *Where Do the Children Play?* (For more information, see www.childrenplay.org.)
- Work with other organizations committed to restoring children's play
- Maintenance of an updated list of resources for parents and educators related to play.

A final resource to assist in our advocacy efforts is Teachers Resisting Unhealthy Children's Entertainment (TRUCE). TRUCE is an association of childhood professionals who work to promote a positive play environment for children. Resources include the Toy Action Guide, the Media Violence Guide, fliers on such topics as television and your child and scary play, and press releases on advocacy issues.

Child's play is a very serious subject. It is an essential element in the normal development of children. As early childhood educators and advocates, we must enable children to explore their world, to develop cultural understandings, to express their thoughts and feelings, and to meet and solve problems. All this can be accomplished through play.

References

Alliance for Childhood. (2005). *Time for play, every day: It's fun and fundamental.* College Park, MD: Author.

Almon, J. (2003). The vital role of play in early childhood education. *Research Bulletin, 8*(2), 4-19. Available from www.waldorflibrary.org/Journal_Articles/RB802.pdf

American Academy of Pediatrics, Committee on Public Education. (1999). Policy statement on media education. *PEDIATRICS, 104*(2), 341-343.

American Academy of Pediatrics. (2002). *Television—How it affects children.* Elk Grove Village, IL: Author. Available from www.aap.org/pubed/ZZZGF8VOQ7C.htm?&sub_cat=1

American Academy of Pediatrics. (2006). *The importance of play in promoting healthy child development and maintaining strong parent-child bonds.* Elk Grove Village, IL: Author. Available from http://www.aap.org/pressroom/playFINAL.pdf.

Arnold, J. C. (2001). Defending childhood—Encouraging children to be themselves. *Child Care Information Exchange,* January/February.

Association for Childhood Education International/Isenberg, J., & Quisenberry, N. (2002). *Play: Essential for all children. A position paper.* Olney, MD: Association for Childhood Education International. Available from www.acei.org/playpaper.htm

Bergen, D. (2002). The role of pretend play in children's cognitive development. *Early Childhood Research & Practice, 4*(1).

Canadian Paediatric Society. (2003). Impact of media use on children and youth. *Paediatrics & Child Health,*

8(5), 301-306.

Condren, L. (2005). *The lost playgrounds.* Available from www.irishhealth.com/index. html?level=4&id=3091

Dettore, E. (2004). A world without play. *Pittsburgh Association for the Education of Young Children Newsletter, 38*(1), 1, 10.

Dramstad, A. (1999). All work and no play . . . In many schools, daily recess goes the way of the inkwell. *NAESP Communicator, 22*(5). Available from www.naesp.org/ContentLoad.do?contentId=132

Elkind, D. (2001). *The hurried child: Growing up too fast too soon* (3rd ed.). New York: Perseus Publishing.

Furlow, B. (1999, March 27). Play's the thing. *New Scientist, 2294,* 28.

Groos, K. (1909). *The play of man.* New York: Appleton.

Illinois Early Learning Project. (2004). *Organized sports and young children.* Available from www.illinoisearlylearning.org/tipsheets/sports.pdf

International Play Association USA. (2006). *What we do.* Available from www.ipausa.org/what.htm

Jordan, A. B., Hersey, J. C., McDivitt, J. A., & Heitzler, C. D. (2006). Reducing children's television-viewing time: A qualitative study of parents and their children. *Pediatrics, 118*(5), 1303-1310.

KidsHealth for Parents. (2005). *Childhood stress.* Available from kidshealth.org/parent/emotions/feelings/stress.html

KidsHealth for Parents. (2005). *How TV affects your child.* Available from www.kidshealth.org/parent/positive/family/tv_affects_child.html

Kraus, R. (1990). *Recreation and leisure in modern society* (4th ed.). New York: HarperCollins College.

Levin, D. (2000). Learning about the world through play. *Early Childhood Today, 15*(3), 56.

Levin, D. (2004, February). Toying with children's health: How the business of play harms children. *Proceedings of Third Annual Stop Commercial Exploitation of Children Summit,* New York.

MacPherson, K. (2004, August 15). Experts concerned about children's creative thinking. *Post-Gazette. com.* Available from www.post-gazette.com/pg/04228/361969.stm

Marcon, R. (2002). Moving up the grades: Relationship between preschool model and later school success. *Early Childhood Research & Practice, 4*(1). Available from http://ecrp.uiuc.edu/v4n1/marcon.html

Montague, A. (1983). *Growing young.* New York: McGraw-Hill.

Olfman, S. (Ed.). (2003). *All work and no play... How educational reforms are harming our preschoolers.* Westport, CT: Praeger Publishers.

Pellegrini, A., & Glickman, C. (1989). The educational role of recess. *Principal, 68*(5), 23-24.

Piaget, J. (1932). *Play, dreams and imitation.* New York: Norton.

Rowlands, F. (1997). The value of play. *Child & Family Canada.* Available from www.cfc-efc.ca/docs/cccf/00003_en.htm

Seefeldt, C. (1995). Play, policy & practice. In E. Klugman (Ed.), *Playing with policy* (pp. 185-194). St. Paul, MN: Readleaf Press.

Self, F. (1996). Making the most of outdoor play. *Child Care Center Connections, 5*(3).

Singer, D. G., Singer, J., Plaskon, S. L., & Schweder, A. E. (2003). A role for play in the preschool curriculum. In S. Olfman (Ed.), *All work and no play... How educational reforms are harming our preschoolers.* Westport, CT: Praeger Publishers.

Sluckin, A. (1981). *Growing up in the playground.* London: Routledge & Kegan Paul.

Sutton-Smith, B. (1971). A syntax for play and games. In R. Herron & B. Sutton-Smith (Eds.), *Child's play* (pp. 298-310). New York: Wiley.

TRUCE. (2003). *Killjoy toys: Experts warn against playthings that snuff out play.* Press release, November 20, 2003. Available from www.allianceforchildhood.net/news/killjoy_toys.htm

Vygotsky, L. (1978). *Mind in society.* Cambridge, MA: Harvard University Press.

Wilson, F. R. (1999). *The hand: How its use shapes the brain, language, and human culture.* New York: Vintage.

Zigler, E. F., Singer, D. G., & Bishop-Josef, S. J. (Eds.). (2004). *Children's play: The roots of reading.* Washington, DC: ZERO TO THREE Press.

A Play-Based Curriculum To Promote Literacy Development
Christine Jeandheur Ferguson

CHAPTER 4

Research has described reading as a social phenomenon (Goodman, 1986; Snow, 1983; Sulzby, 1986). This social nature of the reading process is especially powerful during the early stages of literacy acquisition (Ferreiro, 1986). Therefore, curriculum experts advocate the importance of the dramatic play setting as a context that supports literacy learning as a social process (Davidson, 1996; Stone & Christie, 1996). According to Sluss (2005), a play-based curriculum in the early years can provide a smooth transition into public school. Play consumes much of a young child's time and energy and it is here where reading and writing begin (Ferguson & McNulty, 2006). When provided with a developmentally appropriate play environment that is abundant with print-rich materials and props, children enter their play environment with a natural curiosity to explore the meaning of written language (Ferguson, 2001, Morrow & Rand, 1991; Vukelich, 1991a, 1994). Subsequently, they begin to discover uses for literacy in purposeful and appropriate ways (Vukelich, 1990). In print-rich play environments, young children are observed engaging in collaborative literacy activities with each other and adults, while acting out real-life dramatizations (Neuman & Roskos, 1992). Vygotsky (1978b) maintained that as children engage in make-believe play, they build up stores of represented meanings that are necessary for success in learning to read. Researchers also examine literacy from the child's perspective, which provides understanding about the process of children's literacy behaviors (Kontos, 1986; Roskos, 1988; Strickland & Morrow, 1990; Vukelich, 1990).

In this chapter, the following issues concerning play and literacy development will be explored: 1) the definition of sociodramatic play, 2) the value of sociodramatic play, 3) sociodramatic play and literacy learning, 4) a play-based curriculum to promote literacy development, and 5) a child-constructed sociodramatic play center.

The Definition of Sociodramatic Play

Smilansky (1968) coined the term *sociodramatic play* to define pretend play in a social context. Levy, Wolfgang, and Koorland (1992) define sociodramatic play as "play that involves voluntary social role-taking with others" (p. 246). Piaget defined sociodramatic play as "the most highly developed form of symbolic play between two and seven years of age" (as cited in Warash & Workman, 1993, p. 9). To an extent, sociodramatic play differs from dramatic play. In what is termed *dramatic play*, children pretend on their own as they act out situations, excluding others in the process. They imitate real-life episodes as they draw upon first- or secondhand experiences, using real or imaginary objects. For example, in dramatic play, one child may pretend to be a police officer. Another child may pretend to be a dog, or transform a box into a television. However, when a theme is elaborated upon in cooperation with another participant, and both participants interact through action and speech, the play then becomes sociodramatic play (Christie, 1982; Smilansky & Shefatya, 1990). Sociodramatic play, like dramatic play, involves the use of objects to symbolize objects that are not present. Children exchange information and ideas as they jointly participate in elaborate theme-related play episodes.

Sociodramatic play is one of the most sophisticated types of play engaged in by young children, and it is critical to their cognitive and social development (Berk, 1994; Christie, 1982; Gentile & Hoot, 1983; Smilansky, 1968; Stone, 1995; Warash & Workman, 1993). Children who engage in this type of pretend or imaginative play adopt specific roles and attempt to re-create real-life situations based on their experiences (Christie, 1982). They demonstrate a growing awareness of their social and cultural surroundings and of other children's perspectives as they use symbolic representation to act out interactions (Johnson, Christie, & Yawkey, 1987). Sociodramatic play is an especially rich and complex combination of language and play.

The Value of Sociodramatic Play

Theorists and researchers have differed in their assumptions about sociodramatic play and its purpose. Yet all affirm its significance in the development of intellectual, social, and emotional growth. Sigmund Freud's (1959) psychoanalytic theory emphasizes that sociodramatic play allows children to construct imaginative roles and play out feelings by showing their "inner selves." Through sociodramatic play, children are able to rid themselves of negative feelings that may be associated with traumatic events in their lives. In this way, sociodramatic play can have value as a diagnostic and therapeutic tool, enabling children to express their emotions and release strong feelings (Johnson, Christie, & Yawkey, 1987).

Vygotsky (1978a) asserts that sociodramatic play provides a transitional stage when children use objects to stand for other things (e.g., a stick becomes a horse), thus contributing significantly to the development of abstract, logical thought. Not only are children acting in response to external stimuli, they are also acting in accordance with their internal ideas. This type of response enables the child to act independently of what he actually sees (Creasy, Jarvis, & Berk, 1998). Vygotsky (1976) maintains that, to the casual observer, children's sociodramatic play appears to be free and spontaneous. Yet, this type of play places demands on children to follow specific rules within the context of their play while acting against their immediate impulses. In so doing, children come to understand the social norms and expectations placed on them as they strive to behave appropriately (Berk, 1994).

According to Vygotsky's sociocultural theory, *imaginative play* is learned through social interactions. As children engage in conversations with other children and adults during sociodramatic play, they internalize these interactions, and use them to gain mastery of certain tasks and skills (Smolucha & Smolucha, 1998). Vygotsky (1978a) describes the *zone of proximal development* (ZPD) as "the distance between the actual developmental level as determined by independent problem solving and the level of potential development as determined through problem solving under adult guidance or in collaboration with more capable peers" (p. 86). Vygotsky's ideals state that children learn higher level thinking and problem-solving skills by internalizing interactions through speech with a person or persons who are more knowledgeable (Smolucha & Smolucha, 1998).

Piaget (1962) believes that imaginative play is a developmental process. Based on his theory, children progress through the following four general stages of play: 1) functional play, 2) constructive play, 3) dramatic or symbolic play, and 4) what will change over time from imaginative play into "games with rules." Children bring to pretend play their existing knowledge and skills. Play provides a medium from which children begin to construct new knowledge and assimilate these ideas into their play, which results in new pretend situations. Thus, Piagetian theory stresses that children play an active role in their own cognitive development.

Sociodramatic Play and Literacy Learning

Sociodramatic play also can be defined as *group pretend play* that involves a common goal or theme (Bagley & Klass, 1997) and has been linked to improving social skills, broadening concepts, and the acquisition of knowledge (Bagley, 1994; Berk, 1994; Christie, 1982; Gentile & Hoot, 1983; Rosen, 1974; Smilansky, 1968; Warash & Workman, 1993). As a facilitator of literacy learning, the potential of sociodramatic play has attracted the interests of early childhood educators and led to a number of research studies aimed at encouraging literacy-related play (Christie & Enz, 1992; Einarsdottir, 1996; Morrow & Rand, 1991; Neuman & Roskos, 1991; Roskos, 1988; Schrader, 1990; Vukelich, 1991b). For example, Pellegrini (1980) found that play was a significant predictor of kindergartners' achievement in emergent reading, writing, and language.

Einarsdottir (1996) and Roskos (1988) studied how specifically designed print environments influenced children's literate behaviors during play. Through physical design changes, they created classroom literacy settings that allowed play to become an important context for children's reading and writing. The researchers found that children behaved like readers and writers as they handled paper, wrote stories, and used print and literacy materials in purposeful and meaningful ways.

Morrow (1990) and Christie and Enz (1992) conducted similar studies to determine if the number of children's literate behaviors during their sociodramatic play would increase in type and quantity from physical design changes in preschool classroom play centers to include reading and writing materials. The authors found that teacher guidance, in combination with classroom design changes that included literacy-related materials, supported children's literacy development.

Neuman and Roskos (1992) sought to determine if physical design changes in sociodramatic play centers that included props and literacy-related materials would influence children to demonstrate more sustained and elaborate sequences of literacy in their play. The authors found that children who played with these materials made significant increases in the duration and complexity of literacy-related play.

Children's acquisition of knowledge about print is enhanced through social interactions with more knowledgeable partners. Consistent with Vygotsky's (1978a) sociocultural theory, play creates a zone of proximal development (ZPD) whereby children's learning can be enhanced by interactions with more capable peers. In conjunction with Vygotsky's (1978a) theory, teachers play a vital role in supporting and guiding children as they scaffold their use of these materials.

Christie and Enz (1992), Morrow (1990), Neuman and Roskos (1992), Schrader (1990), Stone and Christie (1996), and Vukelich (1994) utilized Vygotskian (1978a) theory in their studies by including functional experiences with print and literacy-related materials in early childhood classrooms. The researchers linked real-life experiences outside the classroom environment by creating specific theme-related classroom sociodramatic play settings (e.g., restaurant, office, post office, veterinary hospital). These play centers were enriched with print items, literacy-related materials, and authentic props commonly found in real-life settings. The researchers found that children became engaged in social interactions with their peers and adults and demonstrated increases in their literate behaviors.

A Play-based Curriculum To Promote Literacy Development

Substantial research (Christie, 1990; Morrow & Weinstein, 1986; Neuman & Roskos, 1990; Vukelich, 1990, 1991a) has focused on the importance of the sociodramatic play setting as a vehicle for children's literacy learning. A sociodramatic play environment is most valuable when it is stimulating, inviting, and abundant in print-rich materials, realistic props, and manipulatives that are meaningful to children (Ferguson, 1999). This type of play environment provides children with a risk-free context in which to practice their emerging literacy skills, the content to enhance their reading and writing skills, and an engaging mode to support their literacy learning (Fields, Groth, & Spangler, 2004).

"Children need ample time to explore, discover, and become actively involved in play episodes, as well as become familiar with new materials and themes" (Ferguson, 1999, p. 28). According to Christie (1990), young children are more likely to engage in elaborate and sustained dramatic play during 30-minute play periods rather than 15-minute play sessions. Holistic classrooms specifically design free-play time so that children will manipulate, explore, discover, and practice, using a rich array of materials and experiences geared to develop the whole child.

Unfortunately, the push for academics has negatively affected the play-based curriculum in preschool and kindergarten classrooms. Many states mandate that early childhood teachers must spend specific periods of time each day teaching required subjects (Kieff & Casbergue, 2000; Sluss, 2005). Free-play time is often replaced with structured times that emphasize workbooks, worksheets, and skill-and-drill activities. These learning aids not only fail to engage and stimulate young children's minds, they also inhibit children's natural abilities to make sense of print and often lead to frustration and stress (Elkind, 1988). Additionally, "Many parents, the general public, and some teachers and school administrators perceive play as being a fun but rather frivolous activity. Rather, they view play as a nice treat for children who have spent time engaged in more serious learning tasks" (Henniger, 2002, p. 130), or as a tangible reward for completing their work. Yet, research indicates that every aspect of a child's development is enhanced through play. Young children are more likely to construct knowledge and master skills that apply to activities that are meaningful to them (Katz & Chard, 1991). In other words, "Young children still need to play and they need a curriculum that promotes holistic growth and development" (Sluss, 2005, p. 201).

Early childhood educators play a crucial role in developing a high-quality, play-based curriculum that fosters and enhances young children's development. They must consider state guidelines and the educational philosophy of the community, school administrators, and other teachers. Then, they determine which theoretical base and philosophy will guide their choices. More important, they also must be in tune with the individual needs, interests, and developmental levels of the children whom they teach.

The housekeeping center, which sets the stage for sociodramatic play to occur, has traditionally been an integral part of many preschool and kindergarten classrooms. This center typically includes pots and pans, dishes, play food, dolls, dress-up clothes, and an assortment of other play items. (Ferguson, 1999, p. 23)

Oftentimes, this center remains unchanged throughout the school year and has limited, or is devoid of, literacy-related materials. In some preschool and kindergarten classrooms, literacy-related materials are only evident at specific centers, such as the reading and writing centers. Early childhood educators can provide young children with ample opportunities to "leap into literacy" by designing sociodramatic play centers that include authentic props and literacy materials (Ferguson, 1999, p. 23). When play themes are associated with every-day events in young children's lives, they will be more willing to experiment with real-life uses of literacy. For example, by adding place mats, restaurant menus, order forms, pencils and pens, play money, and a cash register, children will be more apt to become engaged in authentic and elaborate literacy activities, such as reading menus, writing restaurant orders, and paying for their meals (Ferguson, 1999).

A Child-Constructed Sociodramatic Play Center

Young children also can be valuable contributors to the physical design of a sociodramatic play environment that focuses on their real-life experiences and interests. For example, one day during Show and Tell, my kindergarten children expressed their keen interest about pets, as described in the excerpt below:

"This is my cat, Shadow," explained Kaylee as she held up a candid photograph of her beloved pet for her kindergarten class to see. "I have two cats!" exclaimed Cameron. "My dog's name is Baby," added Mark. The children's excitement level was contagious as each child shared something about a pet they own, had owned, or wished to own. Each child's story prompted other children to relate their personal stories. Susie, who was familiar with the routine of studying topics of interest, commented, "Let's learn more about pets." (Ferguson, 1999, p. 23)

The children's intense interest about pets led me to launch a play-based project that began with a visit to a local pet store. Field trips offer children firsthand experiences that can expand upon their ideas and knowledge about people and places within their community

photos courtesy of author

Figure 1
Children recorded what they saw at the pet store.

Figure 2
Children drew pictures of pets they saw at the pet store.

Figure 3
Children copied some of the words from pet store signs.

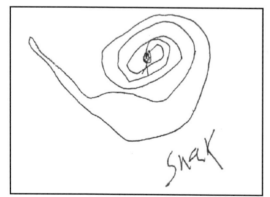

Figure 4
Children wrote words and drew pictures of pets.

(Ferguson, 1999; Ferguson & McNulty, 2006; Van Scoy, 1995).

Prior to the trip, I asked children to predict which pets they might see at the pet store. I also encouraged them to spell pet names as I recorded their responses on the chalkboard. Additionally, the children were provided with a clipboard, paper, and pencil to take the pet store in order to accurately record the pets they found there.

While touring the pet store, children recorded what they saw on their paper (see Figure 1). Some children chose only to draw pictures (see Figure 2), others chose to copy some of the words from store signs (see Figure 3), while still others wrote words and drew pets or pet items they saw (see Figure 4). The children were excited about the numerous animals and reptiles they saw in the pet store and responded with such comments as, "Oooo! I don't like spiders. Yuk!" and "This snake is awesome!" I asked children questions as they walked through each aisle of the store. Some of the questions included, "What type of pet items are these?" and "How do you know?" Many of the children used picture clues to support their answers. For example, some children responded that the picture of the pet was displayed on the pet item (a cat was pictured on a cat food label). Other children sounded out some of the words on the signs and pet items. Still others made attempts to read some of the store signs and pet items. At the conclusion of our pet store visit, the pet store manager, Ms. Patty, contributed the following items to take back to our kindergarten classroom: store signs displaying their logo, pet pamphlets, two pet magazines, store coupons, shopping bags, flyers, and price labels.

At school, the children and I engaged in a classroom discussion about the field trip experience and the unusual pets at the pet store. The children were eager to name the pets they had not predicted finding prior to the field trip. These conversational interchanges helped to clarify and evaluate what children learned as a result of their field trip experience. Then I asked the children, "What should we do with the items Ms. Patty gave us?" The children all began talking at once and excitedly decided, "We want to make a pet store!" "Yeah, let's make a pet store and use the stuff in our pet store." As I presented each item, I questioned the children about the use of the item. For example, in reference to store signs, I asked, "What are these for?" The children responded, "We got to use those to write the name of the pets" and "So we know how much money to pay." I also asked children to identify and list other items they would need to construct a classroom pet store as I listed them on chart paper. The following dialogue took place:

Teacher:	What kinds of things do we need for a pet store?
Peter:	Pets!
Teacher:	What kinds of pets?
Karen:	You know, dogs and cats and stuff.
Kurt:	Yeah, and we gotta have some snakes.
Sally:	Not that big snake. Nuh-uh.
David:	No, silly. We can't have that big snake.
Teacher:	What else could we include in our pet store?
Harry:	Food for the animals.
Susan:	Books about pets.
Teacher:	What else?
Johnny:	More stuff like collars and leashes.
Tonya:	I got a book about doggies.

I invited the children to bring pet items to school the following day. That afternoon, I sent a letter home to parents, explaining the children's idea to extend their interest in pets into the classroom by constructing a kindergarten pet store, and included a variety of suggestions of pet items they may like to contribute. Before dismissing the children, I asked them to think about how they could construct or build their classroom pet store and explained that they would begin construction of their pet store the next day.

The following day, several children arrived at school with their pet(s) and pet item(s). I began group time with a discussion about their contributions and invited children to share them with their peers. Some of their pet items included the following: boxes of dog and cat food, cans of dog and cat food, pet treats, stuffed cats and dogs, a toy hamster in a cage, plastic bags, toy lizards, toy snakes, a stuffed fish, and a book about dogs. I also reminded children to continue to bring pet items daily to add to their pet store. As children shared their pets and pet items individually, I encouraged them to make decisions about the construction of their classroom pet store.

During free-play time, children took the lead in designing and constructing the sociodramatic play area known as the housekeeping center into a pet store. Four girls entered the center and classified and arranged the pet food on the store shelves. Two boys joined them and placed stuffed pets and snakes on top of the toy box. They pretended to be pet owners as they acted out play dramatizations in which they shopped in the pet store.

Over the next three weeks, the children continued to bring various pet items to school to add to the kindergarten pet store. I began group time each day by encouraging children to share their pet items with their classmates. After sharing, children placed their pet items in the pet store. Some of these additional pet items included the following props and literacy materials: a pet calendar, price labels, toy snakes, toy frogs, toy insects, pet treats, hamster food, toy spiders, toy turtles, and a very large white metal bird cage with a stuffed "Tweety-Bird" inside. Parents also were generous in sending other items to school for inclusion in the pet store, such as receipt booklets, books about pets, a digital cash register, and a grocery bag full of empty cans of cat and dog food.

As more and more pet items arrived each day, the children questioned, "Where can we put our stuff?" I explained that they were responsible for making important decisions about the construction of their pet store. Peter asked, "Do we have to keep everything in the housekeeping center?" I asked children what other options they had. Johnny questioned, "Can we move some of it to the next center?" (referring to the block center). Sally responded, "Can we move the puppet stage?" The other children chimed in, "Yeah! Let's do that!" I agreed with the children that there was limited space left in the housekeeping center. It seemed logical to the children to use the space next to the housekeeping center, known as the block center, for their expansion of the pet store.

During free play, four boys worked collaboratively as they moved large blocks in the block center and arranged them to simulate store aisles and shelves (see Figure 5). As Dean

Figure 5
Two boys worked together to build store aisles and shelves.

and Johnny lifted the heavy blocks, Johnny yelled to the other two boys, "Hey guys! These blocks are heavy. I need some help." Two boys joined them as they continued to construct the aisles and design the expansion of the pet store. These aisles served as a display for their pet items. Two of the boys went back and forth between the writing center and pet store center as they made signs for pets, labeling them with pet names and prices (see Figures 6 and 7) and taping them on store shelves. Sally, Dean, and Judd moved the puppet stage from against the wall (where it appeared to serve as a storage shelf) to the dividing area that separated the block and housekeeping center. They placed the digital cash register on the top shelf, pretending that it was the cashier counter. Three girls and one boy busied themselves at the writing center where they worked on price labels (see Figure 8), writing

Figure 6
Pet store signs for pets.

Figure 7
Pet store signs for pet items.

Figure 8
Children work collaboratively on price labels and pet store signs.

numbers and prices and taping them to individual pets and pet items.

One day, during free-play time, Chris exclaimed, "My puppy had an awful accident," as he presented a scrawny brown stuffed dog that was missing a black button eye. "My goodness, what happened to your poor dog?" I asked. Chris replied, "He got his eye poked out with a stick. Can we take him to the pet doctor?" "It's not a pet doctor. It's a veterinarian," replied Susie. "Maybe the veterinarian could come to our classroom," added Kaylee. Taking the cues from the children, I invited a veterinarian to visit the classroom and talk with them about her profession.

The following week, Dr. Smith, her daughter Anna, their pet dog, Fergie, and Dr. Smith's receptionist, Mrs. Kimbrell, visited the classroom. Dr. Smith, dressed in a white laboratory coat with a stethoscope hanging around her neck, began the group discussion by asking how many children had pets. About 20 children raised their hands. Then she explained that pets need medical care just like children do. Dr. Smith and her associates presented a vignette to the children in order to demonstrate daily routines in the veterinarian's office, which involved writing patient charts, talking on the phone with clients, scheduling appointments, examining animals, and writing prescriptions for sick pets. To demonstrate proper canine dental care, Dr. Smith introduced her pet dog, Fergie, to the children and brushed Fergie's teeth while the children laughed and giggled. In conclusion, Dr. Smith and her associates provided the children with authentic materials, such as an appointment book, patient charts, file folders, office stationery, and patient history forms from her office. After the presentation, the children worked together to construct a veterinary clinic beside their pet store. For example, they worked collaboratively on a sign for their clinic (see Figure 9). Additionally, children arranged tables to duplicate what they saw from Dr. Smith's vignette. They dressed in lab coats as they pretended to be veterinarians (see Figure 10). They also

Figure 9
Children constructed a veterinary clinic.

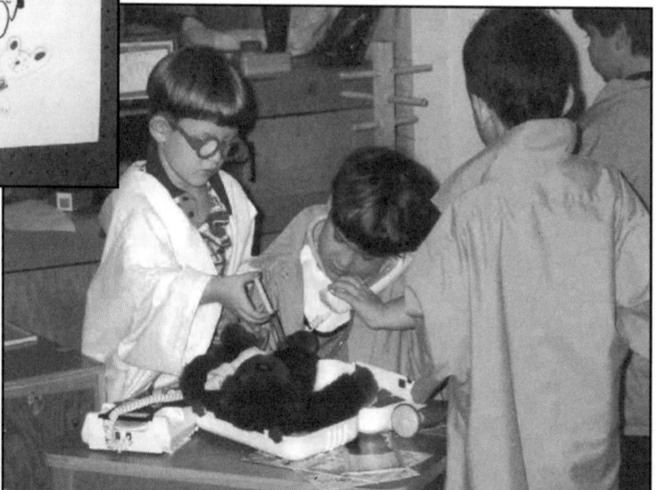

Figure 10
Children dressed in lab coats as they pretended to be veterinarians.

continued to bring their own authentic materials to school, such as stuffed animals, empty medicine bottles, and a doctor's kit to care for sick pets. Table 1 details the list of props and literacy materials that were contributed for use in the pet store and veterinary clinic.

Within a few days, all of the children became actively engaged in the design and construction of the veterinarian clinic. For example, they arranged pet items in specific areas, acted out specific roles, and used the variety of literacy materials (e.g., patient charts, appointment books, folders, thermometers, clipboards, etc.) that were available to them in various learning centers in purposeful ways. Some children wrote receipts for items purchased in the pet store. Others wrote appointments, made notes on patient charts, and wrote prescriptions for sick pets in the veterinary clinic. Additionally, children wrote stories about pets at the writing center (see Figure 11), while others wrote stories about pets on the computer (see Figure 12). Consistent with early literacy stages, these writing samples provided valuable insights

Table 1
Literacy Materials Used by Children During Free Play

Pet Center	Writing Center	Computer Center	Veterinarian's Clinic
Books about pets	Pens and pencils*	computer*	Appointment book*
Pet treats	Markers*	Internet connection*	File folders*
Pet food	Paper*	Word processing program*	Telephone book and telephones*
Notepads	Store signs**		Legal pad
Receipt books	Children's pictionary books*		Pet magazines
Pens and pencils*	Poster-board*		Calculator*
Play money	Staplers*		Prescription pad**
Cash register	Transparencies*		Pens and pencils *
Pet magazines	Post-it notes		Clipboard *
Pet pamphlets**	Pet books		Medicine bottles
Store signs**			Thermometer
Price labels for pets			Toy syringe
Pet calendar			Toy blood pressure gauge
Pet sale flyers**			Pet toys
Pet toys			Patient information sheets**
Store bags**			Play money
Business cards			Pet pamphlets**
Checks			
Credit cards			

Note. Materials not followed by * or ** were contributed by children.
*Materials provided by the teacher   **Materials provided by veterinarian and pet store employees

Figure 11
A child wrote a story about her pet cat.

3-5-98 I lik my cat

Figure 12. A child wrote this story on the computer: Pets: I have a dog, I do. What do you have? Do you have a pet? I do. I hop you have a pet. Wow! You have a pet. Kelly loves pets. I do love pets. I do. I really love pets. I really love pets. Do you really love pets?

pets

i hav a dog i do wht do you hav do you hav a pet I do I hop you hav a pet wow you hav a pet kelly loves pets i do love pets I do I rely love pets i rely love pets do you rely love pets

about children's various ability levels and literacy skills. Social studies, science, math, and language arts were naturally integrated as the students directed their own learning, and I was available as a facilitator to support their learning. The taxonomy of children's literacy activities (see Figure 13) provides a visual representation of children's literate behaviors observed during their sociodramatic play.

Conclusion

Children's interest, excitement, and active engagement related to the theme of "pets" did not wane—in fact, it lasted for four weeks. Through their imaginative efforts, the children took the lead in contributing authentic props and materials that served to enhance and facilitate their literacy learning. They used their problem-solving strategies to design and construct the pet store and veterinary clinic. In addition, they took on more mature approaches as they became engaged in elaborate role-playing within the social contexts of their play. As I observed the children during free-play time, I noticed that object familiarity became important to them as they selected theme-related props and literacy materials that they had

Figure 13
A Taxonomy of Literacy Activities

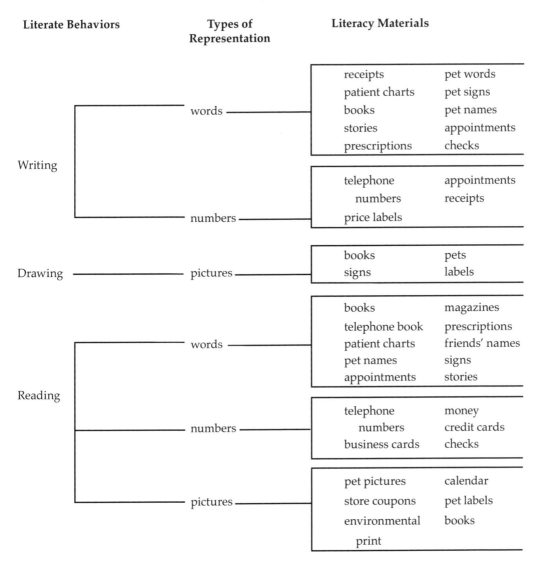

Literate Behaviors	Types of Representation	Literacy Materials	
Writing	words	receipts / patient charts / books / stories / prescriptions	pet words / pet signs / pet names / appointments / checks
	numbers	telephone numbers / price labels	appointments / receipts
Drawing	pictures	books / signs	pets / labels
Reading	words	books / telephone book / patient charts / pet names / appointments	magazines / prescriptions / friends' names / signs / stories
	numbers	telephone numbers / business cards	money / credit cards / checks
	pictures	pet pictures / store coupons / environmental print	calendar / pet labels / books

contributed for the pet store and veterinary clinic. It was interesting to note that the novelty of these props and literacy materials did not diminish; rather, they continued to hold the children's interest for several weeks. The children incorporated their personal props and literacy materials into their play dramatizations in meaningful and purposeful ways.

Literacy-rich sociodramatic play centers offer children authentic and risk-free environments in which to explore and practice their emergent literacy skills. To be effective and meaningful, these centers should be built around children's real-life experiences and interests. Ample time (at least 30 minutes) should be provided for children to engage in meaningful and sustained play episodes within these centers. Children also should be included in the decision-making process regarding what themes to pursue and what kinds of theme-related props and authentic literacy materials should be included in their sociodramatic play centers.

They should be allowed to assist in the design and construction of these play centers. In this way, we can empower children to become autonomous learners. As children explore and make use of literacy materials during their play episodes, they are mastering their conceptual understanding of literacy. " By presenting print in connection with sociodramatic play, early childhood educators will challenge children's creative and intellectual abilities and talents and provide them with sound start for becoming successful readers and writers" (Ferguson, 1999. p. 28).

References

Bagley, D. M. (1994, March). *Housekeeping or thematic sociodramatic play centers: Which is better in the preschool classroom?* Paper presented at the Association for Childhood Education International Annual Conference, New Orleans, LA.

Bagley, D. M., & Klass, P. H. (1997). Comparison of the quality of preschoolers' play in housekeeping and thematic sociodramatic play centers. *Journal of Research in Childhood Education, 12*(1), 71-77.

Berk, L. E. (1994). Vygotsky's theory: The importance of make-believe play. *Young Children, 50*(1), 30-39.

Christie, J. F. (1982). Sociodramatic play training. *Young Children, 37*(4), 25-32.

Christie, J. F. (1990). Dramatic play: A context for meaningful engagements. *The Reading Teacher, 43*(8), 542-545.

Christie, J. F., & Enz, B. (1992). The effects of literacy play interventions on preschoolers' play patterns and literacy development. *Early Education and Development, 3*(3), 205-220.

Creasey, G. L., Jarvis, P. A., & Berk, L. E. (1998). A historical overview of theories of play. In O. N. Saracho & B. Spodek (Eds.), *Multiple perspectives on play in early childhood education* (pp. 7-8, 50-51, 122). Albany, NY: State University of New York Press.

Davidson, J. (Ed.). (1996). *Emergent literacy and dramatic play in early childhood education.* Albany, NY: Delmar Publishers.

Einarsdottir, J. (1996). Dramatic play and print. *Childhood Education, 72*, 352-357.

Elkind, D. (1988). The dynamics of hurrying: Parents. In D. Elkind (Ed.), *The hurried child* (pp. 23-46). Reading, MA: Addison-Wesley Publishing Company.

Ferguson, C. (1999). Building literacy with child-constructed sociodramatic play centers. *Dimensions of Early Childhood, 27*(3), 23-29.

Ferguson, C. (2001). Discovering, supporting, and promoting young children's passions and interests: One teacher's reflections. *Young Children, 56*(4), 6-11.

Ferguson, C. & McNulty, C.P. (2006, Spring). Learning through sociodramatic play. *Kappa Delta Pi Record Online Extra.* Retrieved from www.kdp.org/pdf/publications/ferguson.pdf#search='Learning%20through%20sociodramatic%20play.

Ferreiro, E. (1986). The interplay between information and assimilation in beginning literacy. In W. H. Teale & E. Sulzby (Eds.), *Emergent literacy: Writing and reading* (pp. 15-49). Norwood, NJ: Ablex Publishing Corporation.

Fields, M., Groth, L., & Spangler, K. (2004). Literacy develops through play and experiences. In M. Fields, L. Groth, & K. Spangler (Eds.), *Let's begin reading right* (pp. 44-72). Upper Saddle River, NJ: Pearson Prentice Hall.

Freud, S. (1959). Creative writers and daydreaming. In J. Strackey (Ed.), *The standard edition of the complete psychological works of Sigmund Freud* (Vol. IX) (pp. 141-153). London: Hogarth.

Gentile, L. M., & Hoot, J. L. (1983). Kindergarten play: The foundation of reading. *The Reading Teacher, 36*(4), 436-439.

Goodman, Y. M. (1986). Children coming to know literacy. In W. H. Teale & E. Sulzby (Eds.), *Emergent literacy: Writing and reading* (pp. 1-14). Norwood, NJ: Ablex Publishing.

Johnson, J. E., Christie, J. F., & Yawkey, T. D. (Eds.). (1987). Observing play. *Play and early childhood development* (pp. 148-167). Glenview, IL: Scott Foresman and Company.

Katz, L. & Chard, S. (1991). Engaging children's minds: The project approach.

Kieff, J. E., & Casbergue, R. M. (2000). Fostering language and literacy through playful learning and playful teaching. In J. E. Kieff & R. M. Casbergue (Eds.), *Playful learning and teaching* (pp. 185-208). Needham Heights, MA: Allyn & Bacon.

Kontos, S. (1986). What preschool children know about reading and how they learn it. *Young Children, 42*(1), 58-66.

Levy, A. K., Wolfgang, C. H., & Koorland, M. A. (1992). Sociodramatic play as a method for enhancing the language performance of kindergarten age students. *Early Childhood Research Quarterly, 7*(2), 245-262.

Morrow, L. M. (1990). Preparing the classroom environment to promote literacy during play. *Early Childhood Research Quarterly, 5*(4), 537-554.

Morrow, L. M., & Rand, M. K. (1991). Promoting literacy during play by designing early childhood classroom environments. *The Reading Teacher, 44*(6), 396-402.

Morrow, L. M., & Weinstein, C. S. (1986). Encouraging voluntary reading: The impact of literature program on children's use of library corners. *Reading Research Quarterly, 21*(3), 330-346.

Neuman, S. B., & Roskos, K. (1990). Play, print, and purpose: Enriching play environments for literacy development. *The Reading Teacher, 44*(3), 214-221.

Neuman, S. B., & Roskos, K. (1991). Peers as literacy informants: A description of children's literacy conversations in play. *Early Childhood Research Quarterly, 6,* 233-248.

Neuman, S. B., & Roskos, K. (1992). Literacy objects as cultural tools: Effects on children's literacy behaviors in play. *Reading Research Quarterly, 27*(3), 202-225.

Pellegrini, A. D. (1980). The relationship between kindergartners' play and reading, writing, and language achievement. *Psychology in the School, 17*(4), 530-535.

Piaget, J. (Ed.). (1962). *Play, dreams and imitation in childhood* (C. Gattegno & F. M. Hodgson, Trans.). New York: W. W. Norton & Company.

Rosen, C. E. (1974). The effects of sociodramatic play on problem-solving behavior among culturally disadvantaged preschool children. *Child Development, 45*(4), 920-927.

Roskos, K. (1988). Literacy at work in play. *The Reading Teacher, 41*(6), 562-565.

Schrader, C. T. (1990). Symbolic play as a curricular tool for early literacy development. *Early Childhood Research Quarterly, 5*(1), 79-103.

Sluss, D. J. (2005). Supporting play in kindergarten classrooms. In D. J. Sluss (Ed.), *Supporting play: Birth through eight* (p. 197-236). Clifton Park, NY: Thompson Delmar Learning.

Smilansky, S. (Ed.). (1968). *The effects of sociodramatic play on disadvantaged preschool children* (pp. 7-18, 71-85, 94-95). New York: Wiley.

Smilansky, S., & Shefatya, L. (Eds.). (1990). *Facilitating play: A medium for promoting cognitive, socio-emotional, and academic development in young children* (p. 22). Gaithersburg, MD: Psychosocial & Educational Publications.

Smolucha, L., & Smolucha, F. (1998). The social origins of the mind: Post-Piagetian perspectives on pretend play. In O. N. Saracho & B. Spodek (Eds.), *Multiple perspectives on play in early childhood education* (pp. 34-58). Albany, NY: State University of New York Press.

Snow, C. E. (1983). Literacy and language: Relationships during the preschool years. *Harvard Educational Review, 53*(2), 165-187.

Stone, S. J. (1995). Wanted: Advocates for play in the primary grades. *Young Children, 50*(6), 45-54.

Stone, S. J., & Christie, J. F. (1996). Collaborative literacy learning during sociodramatic play in a multiage (K-12) primary classroom. *Journal of Research in Childhood Education, 10*(2), 123-133.

Strickland, D. S., & Morrow, L. M. (1990). The daily journal: Using language experience strategies in an emergent literacy curriculum. *The Reading Teacher, 43*(6), 422-423.

Sulzby, E. (1986). Writing and reading: Signs of oral and written language organization in the young child. In W. H. Teale & E. Sulzby (Eds.), *Emergent literacy: Writing and reading* (pp. 50-89). Norwood, NJ: Ablex Publishing.

Van Scoy, I. J. (1995). Trading the three R's for the four E's: Transforming curriculum. *Childhood Education, 72,* 19-23.

Vukelich, C. (1990). Where's the paper? Literacy during dramatic play. *Childhood Education, 66,* 205-209.

Vukelich, C. (1991a). Materials and modeling: Promoting literacy during play. In J. F. Christie (Ed.), *Play and early literacy development* (pp. 215-232). Albany, NY: State University of New York Press.

Vukelich, C. (1991b). Play and assessment: Young children's knowledge of the functions of writing. *Childhood Education, 68,* 205-209.

Vukelich, C. (1994). Effects of play interventions on young children's reading of environmental print. *Early Childhood Research Quarterly, 9*(2), 153-170.

Vygotsky, L. S. (1976). Play and its role in the mental development of the child. In J. Bruner, A. Jolly, & K. Syulva (Eds.), *Play—Its role in development and evaluation* (pp. 537-554). New York: Basic Books.

Vygotsky, L. S. (1978a). Interaction between learning and development. In M. Cole, V. John-Steiner, S. Scribner, & E. Souberman (Eds.), *Mind in society: The development of higher psychological processes* (pp. 79-91). Cambridge, MA: Harvard University Press.

Vygotsky, L. S. (1978b). The role of play in development. In M. Cole, V. John-Steiner, S. Scribner, & E. Souberman (Eds.), *Mind in society: The development of higher psychological processes* pp. 92-104). Cambridge, MA: Harvard University Press.

Warash, B. G., & Workman, M. (1993). All life's a stage: Children dictate and reenact personal experiences. *Dimensions of Early Childhood, 21*(4), 9-12.

The Shaping of Children's Cultural Identities Through Play
Carol McNulty

Chapter 5

Children's lives are consumed by play. In fact, some tout play as the most important pursuit of children (Bentzen, 2005). Although play assumes numerous forms, has varied explanations, and can have a myriad of purposes, the aspect of play as a way for children to develop their social and cultural identities cannot be understated. It is through play that children learn from their peers and become subject to the world's reactions. Indeed, play has been deemed the "dominant socializing agent for children's social competence and identity development" (Cooper, 1996, p. 2). As children try to establish who they are and how they fit into the world around them, play becomes an essential tool. Children move between reality, fantasy, and everywhere in between as they "reveal dominant ideological assumptions about categories of individuals and the relations between them" (Dyson, 1996, p. 472). This chapter examines some of the ways in which children shape their social and cultural identities through play. First, we explore the power of play in developing racial identity, followed by an explanation of young children's curiosities about race. Then we track the development of gender-role stereotypes and look at specific considerations for children of gay and lesbian parents. Finally, we delve into the roles of the media in children's play and the role of adults in interpreting play actions.

The Power of Play in Developing Racial Identity

Among other benefits, play affords children the opportunity to engage in cognitive "work." Children's early childhood experiences are powerful in shaping their understanding of culture. As children engage in play, they are able to negotiate cognitive conflicts and work toward resolutions of emotional struggles. One particularly powerful component of this cultural strife is that it helps children develop ideas about racial identity. Some research indicates that children as young as 3 years old begin to form notions about their own and others' race (Banks, 1993). These early developments of cultural and socio-identities are significantly influenced by those people with whom they interact most frequently—particularly their parents, caregivers, and teachers (Rossi & Rossi, 1990). As adults, parents, and teachers, we share a responsibility for the cultural and socio-identity development of children. Therefore, it is imperative that positive experiences with other cultures are provided in order to help children form sensitive perceptions of others (Swick, Boutte, & van Scoy, 1995). Adults, not children, need to assume the responsibility in preparing the foundation for multicultural sensitivity and create experiences that will help children value cultural diversity (Swick et al.). Children's racial identities often are enacted in play, and thus provide observers a window by which to view this development. Observing children's play provides adults an opportunity to learn about how they are experiencing and perceiving issues of race and culture. Young children are naturally curious about race, and often use play as one way to mediate their understandings of it. Play, then, offers adults a unique mode by which to discuss race and other aspects of culture, in a very natural way.

Young Children's Curiosities About Race

Young children are naturally curious about race, particularly when they are confronted with differences. When young children encounter disequilibrium, they tend to search for meaning. In trying to make sense of ethnic differences, children often focus on the concrete aspect of a person's skin color. Such meaning-making is a natural extension of young children's stage of cognitive development, in which the concrete and tangible take precedence over all else. Anyone who has worked closely with young children will confirm that in an attempt to explain differences (for example, in skin color), children often point to events in their own lives that they feel may help explain the color differences. One example of such explanations comes from my own kindergarten teaching experiences. When faced with her peer's question of "Why is your skin darker than mine?," Tia, a female, African American student, replied simply, "God colored me with a different colored crayon than you, that's all." In this account, Tia attempted to explain her understanding of racial differences by using the tools and language of her (and her peer's) everyday experiences of coloring with crayons.

Although Tia was seemingly "comfortable in her own skin," and appeared confident in her explanation of differences, children may not always be satisfied with the explanations they are given about differences in skin tones. In her book *Why Are All the Black Kids Sitting Together in the Cafeteria?*, Beverly Tatum (1997) offers a contrasting example of a preschooler explaining racial differences, based on life experiences. Tatum's young African American son is told by his Euro-American peer that his darker skin is caused by drinking too much chocolate milk (p. 33). Confused by this explanation, he searches for more information and asks his mother's opinion, whereby she explains that he simply has more melanin in his skin. While childish questions and explanations about racial differences are developmentally appropriate and even predictable, adults and children can be confused, misguided, and even angered by responses they consider inappropriate. For this reason, adults often see the need to suppress such comments and questions for fear of embarrassment. Because many adults are not comfortable discussing issues of race and culture, particularly when these conversations may be overheard, this "uncomfortable feeling" may be extended to children, who quickly learn that discussions of race and cultural are topics to be avoided. Thus, it cannot be surprising when children grow into adults who feel neither prepared for nor comfortable discussing issues of race and culture.

Play offers a rich opportunity for children of various races to negotiate and experiment with their understandings of race and ethnicity. Through play, children are able to act out cultural norms, make sense of the experiences around them, and experiment with different types of roles and relationships. Adults viewing these interactions can learn a great deal about how children are interpreting their environment and what they are learning from their influences.

In much the same way as children learn to avoid conversations with adults about race, stereotypes are transmitted to children at a very early age. Images and self-images of race, ethnicity, social class, and gender make their way into children's experiences daily. Through interactions with adults, other children, and the media, children are constantly learning about the world around them. Inevitably, stereotypes creep into their experiences, which ultimately are also enacted in play.

The Development of Gender Roles

In the peer culture of preschool, gender plays an important role, as it defines two categories of membership: female or male (Corsaro, 1997). Gender is a characteristic that seems to permeate children's daily lives (Liang, 2003), and imposes stereotypes, even at an early age. Even before birth, parents and adults quickly begin to discriminate between the genders. Expectant parents often decorate nurseries differently, depending on whether they are expecting a girl or a boy. Once born, the gender identification seems only to become more ingrained. For example, male infants' parents often use "rough and tumble" play more frequently than do parents of female infants (Snoddy, Jones, & Christian, 1993). Boys and girls, even as young as 2 years old, have shown "gender appropriate" activities in their play, and have been rewarded for "gender appropriate play" by both adults and peers (Snoddy et al.). Children's understanding of "gender appropriateness" often is evident by their choice of toys and by how they play. By age 3, children already exhibit a strong gender identification that is solidified through the environment and the people with whom they interact (Snoddy et al.). These early experiences are imperative to shaping the way they will perceive the environment and organize their experiences of gender. As children develop, they "try on" roles of gender, a characteristic of a developmental stage that is appropriate for all young children. Most preschool and kindergarten teachers are quite used to seeing boys in their dramatic play centers don dresses, scarves, or other "typical female" attire.

Equally as important as *what* children play, is *with whom* they play. These interactions help them formulate their interpretations of gender. Young children often choose to play with same-gender peers (Liang, 2003); in fact, gender segregation has been found to increase among 5- to 6-year-olds more than with 3- to 5-year-olds (Corsaro, 1997; Thorne, 1993). The tendency to be accepted by same-sex peers often increases from the preschool years to the middle elementary years (Snoddy et al., 1993) as peers begin to assume an important focus in a child's life. In an ethnographic study conducted by Dyson (1996), who looked specifically at the role of superheroes in play, she notes that when children improvised in play settings, they often relied upon stereotypical gender roles—frequently drawing upon media sources. Other research (e.g., James, 1993; Thorne, 1993) supports the finding that when children are left to play uninhibited, that play is heavily reliant on traditional gender divisions. Children quickly mirror society's messages that males possess power and are strong, brave, and aggressive, while females are compliant, nurturing, weak, dependent, and affectionate (Carter, 1993; Snoddy et al.).

Adults who are privileged to observe this play may have unique opportunities to discuss gender roles and stereotypes as children work to understand gender issues. By examining play, adults may explore how children perceive gender by asking themselves such questions as:

Do girls and boys
- Have rigid or changeable notions about family roles during play?
- Have static or dynamic ideas about gender personality characteristics?
- Dress primarily along traditional gender lines, or do they assume many roles?
- Play with toys that are considered "gender appropriate," or do they experiment?
- Define peers by gender identification to peers ("You can't do that—you're a boy/girl"), or do they seek to determine peers' interests and abilities?
- Play and interact in mixed-gender situations?

As with the formation of ideas about race, adults and professionals should be concerned about their own roles in how children view gender. Adults often hold the power to help break or establish traditional gender boundaries by their interactions with children. Yet many adults are unaware of, or are uncomfortable with, the developmental stage in which children are not rigid in their gender identification. Often unknowingly, they interfere and impose what they consider to be "gender appropriate behavior," even when children are engaged in fantasy play. Interactions with children (both verbal and nonverbal) assume an essential role in how children see their membership in a gender group. Adults often transmit powerful messages about gender by the toys, peers, and themes with which they allow their children to play. However, even adults who are careful to present children with gender-neutral roles may not be able to fully shelter children from the negative images they receive elsewhere, such as the media. Outside influences can be particularly damaging for some groups of children.

Considerations for Children of Gay and Lesbian Parents

Despite substantial research that supports the notion that children who grow up with one or two gay and/or lesbian parents fare as well in emotional, cognitive, social, and sexual functioning as do children of heterosexual parents (Perrin, 2002), the media, certain political groups, and other people often portray negative images of such nontraditional families. Consequently, children growing up in gay and lesbian households may be subject to more pressures and challenges than children who grow up in more traditional family configurations, simply due to the effects of stigmatization and discrimination (Perrin, 2002; Ray & Gregory, 2001). Because many pockets of society are still not accepting of nontraditional families, evidenced in part by their lack of institutional privilege (Oswald, 2002), it can be more challenging for children of gay and lesbian parents to develop positive self-esteem in the process of forming cultural identities (Carter, 1993). Carter relates four ways in which society works to undermine the self-esteem of children of gay and lesbian parents:

1. Hearing and seeing no examples of your individual or group identity
2. Hearing and seeing negative, stereotypical, or untrue representations of your life
3. Having to keep secrets to feel safe
4. Having repeated experiences of being labeled a victim, rather than empowered to act in one's behalf (p. 4).

Many situations may perpetuate these components, and therefore present additional challenges to students. Even schools often fail to meet the needs of students with regard to nontraditional family configurations (Rubin, 1995; Van Wormer & McKinney, 2003). For example, a common theme in the early years of school is the discussion of family. Some children (including not only those whose parents are gay or lesbian, but also those who are adopted or are from varying circumstances) may find it uncomfortable to continually talk about families and answer questions about their families (Ray & Gregory, 2001), as they may have unanswered questions themselves. Young children, especially, may become confused by peer interactions (Ray & Gregory) or may not feel prepared to answer others' questions about family structures (Carter, 1993). Teachers need to be sensitive to children's family dynamics and be familiar with their circumstances so they will not perpetuate any feelings of discomfort or loneliness for those children who already may feel somewhat distanced from their peers because of their non-typical family status. Educators should relish the opportunity to prepare themselves and the curriculum for more inclusive perspectives around nontraditional families (Wallace, 2000).

Just as with children of heterosexual parents, children of homosexual parents come from a myriad of circumstances. Gay and lesbian households consist of two-parent homes, single-parent homes, and children who live in two households. Carter (1993) suggests that in helping children form positive identities, it is imperative for educators to reflect upon their own biases, as well as research specific information about children's family structure—for example, what are the family's beliefs, traditions, and celebrations; how are family members referred to by name; and who else is important in the child's life? In this way, educators can use the information in class conversations about families to better reflect the individual's situation. Securing materials, such as posters, photographs, magazines, books, and teacher-made resources, for the classroom that reflect different kinds of families, also will help children develop positive identities (Carter, 1993; Rubin, 1995).

As previously noted, adults are often interested in children's "gender appropriate" play behaviors. Children who play in such "appropriate ways" tend to be rewarded by peers and adults; those who do not often are criticized or left to play alone (Snoddy et al., 1993). Such circumstances can be particularly poignant for children of gay and lesbian parents. Homophobic attitudes are often reinforced during play; when children assume nontraditional gender roles, they often receive messages that their behaviors are "wrong." Many adults are uncomfortable when children experiment with cross-dressing (Carter, 1993) or play with toys that are considered to belong to another gender group. Ironically, in most cases, such experimentation has little connection to the child's future sexual orientation, but rather serves as a means for employing the child's imagination. The process of adults responding to masculine and feminine behavior begins very early on, perhaps as early as infancy, and this process is continued by educators and peers as the child matures. Adult reactions may elicit harmful effects of stifling imagination and experimentation, which, in turn, may perpetuate feelings of homophobia, and may send messages to children of gay and lesbian parents that their families are "wrong." Such messages contribute to children's negative self-images and hinder their self-acceptance (Carter, 1993).

As previously noted, because of their nontraditional status, children of gay and lesbian parents are especially susceptible to the outside views and perceptions that are imposed upon them. One of the strongest forces with which children must contend is that of the media.

The Role of the Media in Children's Play

The media, undoubtedly, plays a dominant role in the transmission of stereotypes. Children are not impervious to these influences; in fact, observations of children's play reflect the severity of these circumstances. Cooper (1996) argues that while play was once limited to life experiences, it is now very heavily influenced by media-defined images. Children often may look to the media to define who they are. Some children, more than others, may be damaged by the images they view through the media.

For example, children of the minority culture may not see themselves reflected as often, or as accurately, as their majority-culture counterparts in the media. Such omissions and inaccuracies can undermine self-esteem (Carter, 1993; Rubin, 1995) and prevent children from developing positive cultural identities. Such reflections may be reinforced in play when other children and adults "act out the script" (Cooper, 1996). With the pervasiveness of television and the increase in child care outside of the home, external influences on a child's identity formation become increasingly noteworthy. Children of color often experience a tension between behavioral cues that are valued at home and those that are valued at school, particularly when their teachers are of the dominant culture (Cooper, 1996). Cooper notes that,

in monoethnic play, the race of characters does not matter. Anyone can be anything, since we are all brown and the characters portrayed in the media are typically white. When the play is integrated, this does not happen. White children are quick to remind children of color that you can't be "so and so" because you are not white. (p. 9)

Cooper explains this dynamic as a means by which white children do not necessarily try to exclude children from play, but rather as a way that they exert their own realities—realities that are often reinforced through the media.

The Role of the Media in Adult Reactions to Play

The media, of course, not only influences children, but adults as well. Adults' expectations are influenced by the media images of minority students' behaviors. For example, the media often portrays minorities as criminals; therefore, teachers may unknowingly try to squelch aggressive behaviors of minority students, or be overly sensitive to certain play behaviors that are not part of their own cultural norm (Cooper, 1996). Many behavioral views are culturally bound; minority students placed with teachers of the majority culture may have very different notions of appropriateness. For example, some cultures may view aggression as taking care of oneself, while others may view it as a negative trait altogether (Cooper, 1996). Depending on a child's background, and how that may or may not match up to the adult's, that child may be either rewarded or punished for acting according to his or her own cultural norms. Such interactions certainly influence what the child comes to view as appropriate or not. When there is a mismatch between "home rules" and "school rules," children are likely to become confused and even frustrated, until they are cognitively able to discern the difference between the two sets of rules of which they are a part. Because of this influence, obviously, the role of adults in analyzing interactions and play is of utmost importance.

Although adults from varying cultural groups may view the importance of play differently (Cooper, 1996), most would agree that teachers and parents can and should provide healthy modeling for positive cultural attitudes. Because the adult role is so imperative to children's formations of healthy cultural and socio-identities, adults need to be prepared to provide positive experiences for children. Below, several practical ways for adults and educators to provide such positive experiences are listed and then described.

- Involve family members in the curriculum
- Use a variety of resources for a variety of purposes
- Choose toys that are free of gender suppositions
- Provide a myriad of play experiences for children.

Involving family members in the curriculum is a simple way to make sure that children's experiences are represented, and represented accurately. Asking family members to participate in school functions also allows other children to experience different families, cultures, and traditions and may serve to break stereotypes that were formerly introduced. Not only are children's experiences validated, they are also celebrated, while also contributing to the academic development of the students.

Using a variety of resources, such as literature, classroom materials and displays, and music can serve a variety of purposes. First, it allows children of all walks of life to see themselves reflected in their surroundings. It also creates a social norm in which children become used to interacting with people and resources that do not necessarily always reflect their own experiences. Literature is an excellent springboard to this end. Adults can choose literature that represents people of varying cultures, in a variety of circumstances. Adults must be careful to choose books that depict ethnic minorities of varied socio-economic classes, nontraditional gender roles, nontraditional family configurations, and cultures in both historical and contemporary time periods. Adults can be good consumers of literature by examining the books for possible stereotypes, hidden or explicit messages about roles, subtle messages about norms, and the ways in which the text and pictures depict people and their situations. Varied resources are likely to promote discussion among children about similarities and differences among people. Swick et al. (1995) suggest bringing in props, such as clothing and hair products, as a way to have children naturally engage in conversations about differences and similarities among people. Traditional dress of other cultures will allow students to experiment with cultures and may extend their thinking beyond typical Western cultures. Displaying daily artifacts (such as eating utensils) also may help children to develop an understanding of, or an interest in, cultural differences. Listening to music or experimenting with dance from another culture may promote children's interests in learning about cultures other than their own.

Parents who wish to raise children in a non-sexist environment may choose toys, clothes, and room decorations that are functional and age-appropriate and not completely gender-specific. They also may promote nontraditional gender roles by allowing children of both genders to "get dirty" and be active. Likewise, they can provide toys such as blocks and coloring tools to children of both genders to help them develop spatial analytic skills and small motor skills (Snoddy et al., 1993).

Most important, adults are responsible for providing children with experiences that will stretch their minds and force them to consider experiences and circumstances not readily available within their own households. Exposure to new ideas and varying modes of doing things helps children to reduce the barrier of "us" versus "them" and allows children to become naturally more accepting of differences.

Play, undoubtedly, is a leading force in children's lives. It allows for the expansion of cognitive abilities, physical development, and the conciliation of peer relations. Through individual effort, peer interactions, and adult reaction, play assumes a critical stance in influencing the social and cultural identities of children. Children use play as a venue for negotiating their positions in the world and thereby solidifying their cultural identities. Adults, and their reactions to play, likewise play an important role in establishing the rules of appropriateness and the norms. Close examination of our own cultural and social identities as adults helps us more fully realize the ramifications of our interactions with children, as they incorporate play as a means to negotiate this complicated terrain.

References

Banks, J. (1993). Multicultural education for young children: Racial and ethnic attitudes and their modification. In B. Spodek (Ed.), *Handbook of research on the education of young children* (pp. 236-250). New York: Macmillan.

Bentzen, W. R. (2005). *Seeing young children: A guide to observing and recording behavior* (5th ed.). Clifton Park, NY: Thomson.

Carter, M. (1993, December). *Supporting the growing identity and self-esteem of children in gay and lesbian families.* Paper presented at the Annual Conference of the National Association for the Education of Young Children, Anaheim, CA. (ERIC Document Reproduction Service No. ED 377985)

Cooper, R. M. (1996). The role of play in the accultural process. *Topics in Early Childhood Education, 2,* 2-11.

Corsaro, W. A. (1997). *The society of childhood.* Thousand Oaks, CA: Pine Forge Press.

Dyson, A. H. (1996). Cultural constellations and childhood identities: On Greek gods, cartoon heroes, and the social lives of schoolchildren. *Harvard Educational Review, 66*(3), 471-495.

James, A. (1993). *Childhood identities: Self and social relationships in the experience of the child.* Edinburgh, UK: Edinburgh University Press.

Liang, C. (2003, April). *Male/female relationships inside and outside of play in a working-class Taiwanese preschool.* Paper presented at the Society for Research in Child Development, Tampa, FL. (ERIC Document Reproduction Service No. ED 478647)

Oswald, R. F. (2002). Resilience within the family networks of lesbians and gay men: Intentionality and redefinition. *Journal of Marriage and Family, 64*(2), 374-383.

Perrin, E. (2002). Coparent or second-parent adoption by same-sex parents. *Pediatrics, 109,* 341-344.

Ray, V., & Gregory, R. (2001). School experiences of the children of lesbian and gay parents. *Family Matters,* Winter(59), 28-34.

Rossi, S., & Rossi, P. (1990). *Of human bonding.* New York: Basic Books.

Rubin, S. A. (1995). *Children who grow up with gay or lesbian parents: How are today's schools meeting this 'invisible' group's needs?* (ERIC Document Reproduction Service No. ED 386290)

Snoddy, V., Jones, K., & Christian, L. G. (1993, March). *A study of stereotyping of infants and toddlers.* Paper presented at the Southern Early Childhood Association, Biloxi, MS. (ERIC Document Reproduction Service No. ED 360089)

Swick, K. J., Boutte, G., & van Scoy, I. (1995). *Family involvement in early multicultural learning.* (ERIC Document Reproduction Service No. ED 380240)

Tatum, B. (1997). *Why are all the black kids sitting together in the cafeteria? And other conversations about race.* New York: Basic Books.

Thorne, B. (1993). *Gender play: Girls and boys in school.* New Brunswick, NJ: Rutgers University Press.

Van Wormer, K., & McKinney, R. (2003). What schools can do to help gay/lesbian/bisexual youth: A harm reduction approach. *Adolescence, 38*(151), 409-420.

Wallace, B. C. (2000). A call for change in multicultural training at graduate schools of education: Education to end oppression and for social justice. *The Teachers College Record, 102*(6), 1086-1111.

CHAPTER 6

THE ARTS AND PLAY(FULNESS)
Howard Booth, Linda Ehrlich, & Elizabeth Deasy

"Art: The urge to play"

—Friedrich von Schiller

Young children are primed for learning and are greatly accepting of most art forms. Strong evidence exists that early arts experiences have an impact on all aspects of a child's learning and development and that, in many ways, "earlier is better" (Isenberg & Jalongo, 1996). The early childhood years thus present both a unique opportunity and a unique challenge; a part of that challenge is to engage and support all who care for and educate young children in making the arts an integrated and vital part of their earliest experiences.

Young children are not just eager to learn. Evidence suggests that they are, in fact, *compelled* to learn (Newberger, 1997). As a result of new research on the development of young children's brains, we know that early experience not only has a psychological impact on development, but also physically creates neural connections that allow a child to learn and process information effectively (Shore, 1997). The arts give children the opportunity to use more than one avenue for learning and to make connections among different parts of the brain. They also develop and strengthen the imagination, develop critical thinking, and refine cognitive and creative skills (Jensen, 1998).

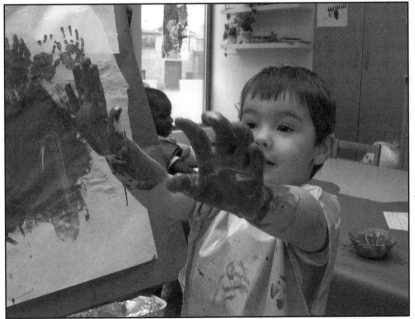

photos courtesy of authors

The arts are an integral part of "best practices," because they are a natural way to support young children's growth across all domains, including:

Cognitive Development, which:
- Allows children to contrast and compare, think independently, make decisions, associate related information and ideas, sequence events, make predictions, understand cause and effect, and communicate ideas nonverbally
- Supports the development of early literacy skills as children move from concrete to abstract thinking and the use of symbols
- Strengthens problem-solving and critical-thinking skills, adding to overall academic achievement and school success
- Motivates and engages children in learning, stimulates memory, facilitates understanding, enhances symbolic communication, promotes relationships, and provides avenues for building competence
- Connects to individual strengths and the developmental growth of every child and is proven to help level the "learning field" across socioeconomic boundaries
- Teaches children such life skills as developing an informed perception, articulating a vision, building self-confidence and self-discipline, developing the ability to imagine possible outcomes, and accepting responsibility to complete tasks from start to finish.

Physical Development, which:
- Engages children's senses
- Increases body awareness
- Enhances gross and fine motor skills and coordination.

Social and Emotional Development, which:
- Invites play partners, whether adults or other children
- Gives children a way to build bridges with others who are different from them
- Nurtures important values, including team-building skills, respecting alternative viewpoints, and appreciating and being aware of different cultures and traditions
- Develops a sense of craftsmanship, quality task performance, and goal-setting—skills needed to succeed in the classroom and beyond
- Provides an outlet for children's emotions, allowing them to integrate experiences and achieve mastery over strong feelings.

Howard Gardner's work on multiple intelligences (cited in Murfee, 1995) points out the value that the arts can play in supporting children's learning:

The arts can play a crucial role in improving students' ability to learn because they draw on a range of intelligences and learning styles, not just the linguistic and logical-mathematical intelligences upon which most schools are based. (p. 7)

Finally, a developmentally appropriate curriculum is process-driven and relationship-based, so its impact on academic performance is often underestimated and undervalued. Arts programs can offer alternatives to more traditionally academic, formal ways of approaching relationships, outcomes, and perceptions.

The Arts and Play(fulness)

We know that "art," understood as spontaneous creative play, is what young children naturally do—singing, dancing, drawing, and role-playing (Arts Education Partnership, 1998). We also know that the arts engage all the senses and involve a variety of modalities, including the kinesthetic, auditory, and visual.

Most important, both play and art are open-ended processes that allow children to express emotion, thoughts, and solve problems without adult-directed structure or intervention. Through play and art, children can create a complex imaginary world, with other children as partners, in which they can explore angry feelings, role play, share, resolve differences with friends, and solve problems—all within a world they can create, control, and change.

Play and art also allow children to enjoy a pure exploration of materials. The materials used for their experiences, whether clay, paint, fabric, sand, water, wooden blocks, or manipulative toys, encourage free and open investigation. These materials have no set configuration, constraints, or solution. They can be whatever children want and need them to be. Elliot Eisner (2002) draws on the work of Johan Huizinga, who looked at elements of play in culture, to conclude::

The arts have an important role to play in refining our sensory system and cultivating our imaginative abilities. Indeed, the arts provide a kind of permission to pursue qualitative experience in a particularly focused way and to engage in the constructive exploration of what the imaginative process may engender. In this sense, the arts in all their manifestations are close to attitude in play. (p. 4)

Play and the arts are essential ways that children use to communicate, express feelings, think, and explore the world and their relationship to it. Both art and play support the ways that children learn most effectively, namely:

- From concrete to abstract
- Sensory-based and hands-on
- Building on prior experiences.

Finally, art is a natural part of play. Young children, as they play in the dramatic play area, sing songs; dance on stages built from blocks; perform plays they spontaneously create with peers; make signs, drawings, and symbols to illustrate; and share. The arts deepen and enrich their play experiences.

Supporting Play(fulness) and the Arts in the Classroom

Educators' role in supporting young children's creativity starts with their personal sense of joy and playfulness. Educators must bring their own sense of curiosity, awe, and creativity into the classroom. More important, they must recognize that art is an area where children may lead the process.

Art is a form of self-expression. As such, it cannot be an imitation of an educator's design. The educator's role in "doing art" with young children is to offer materials and/or activities, and then support children in their creative explorations and interpretations.

Visual art experiences can include explorations of a wide range of paints, colors, brushes, papers, crayons, chalks, pencils, modeling clays, collage materials, wood, fabric, sponges,

kitchen utensils, cotton balls . . . the list is endless. An imaginative educator can mix and match materials to suit every child's interests and developmental level. Let's also consider "materials" in a broader sense, as in "anything we use to stimulate development." Materials, in this case, can include the environment and the people in it. A visually appealing mobile, a new painting, or a textured wall hanging that the children can touch—all of these would be materials in the environment.

When the teacher supports the child, the child feels acceptance. He or she knows it is safe to continue to explore. As children choose materials and decide how to use them, they gain confidence in their abilities. Children learn to accept the limits imposed by the materials. Even if something doesn't turn out as expected, children learn to accept responsibility and to be flexible in their thinking.

Music and movement are included among the arts and play, of course. Even newborns respond to musical sounds. They like being held and rocked. Parents often sing to their babies as they carry them in their arms. These are the babies' earliest music and movement experiences. Educators can enhance the child's musical awareness with a high-quality tape or CD player and a range of recorded music and instruments from around the world. A music area should include not only music for children, but also classical, folk, jazz, rock 'n roll, etc.; musical instruments and other sources of sound; an open space for movement; possibly a mirror (for watching the movement); and props, such as puppets, scarves, and hoops. As with the visual arts, the educator can supply materials and support the child's exploration.

Many educators are uncomfortable using the arts in the ways described above with very young children. They don't like the extra mess that comes with paints and collages. Many feel that they cannot sing well, or they don't like to move. Some people think of art as something outside themselves. In fact, all of us have the capacity to experience art from within ourselves. Let go of preconceived notions of what art should look or sound like. The process of doing with intentionality is what counts. The process is the enriching part, for teachers as well as for children. The arts are universal—an important part of all societies and cultures. They reflect a culture's values and beliefs. Therefore, they play an important part in any curriculum. Educators can support exploration of the arts and play(fulness) by:

- *Establishing an arts area that is ready for spontaneous creative play.* Make a variety of arts materials and tools available, such as paints, brushes, markers, props for theatrical play, and tactile materials (fabrics, wood pieces, recycled packing materials)—anything that is interesting to touch, move, arrange, or build with. Keep an open space for free movement. Have a CD player on hand, as well as music from a variety of genres, places, and times.
- *Facilitating the simultaneous engagement of several sensory realms.* For example, provide music, a large sheet of paper for the floor, and paint for the children's feet. The children will hear and interpret music in the form of movement, printing, and painting. Such processes connect the children's visual, kinesthetic, and auditory realms.
- *Observing carefully and supporting each child's unique way of responding to materials, processes, and sensations.* Children's artistic play naturally evolves in the way that is best for each child. Don't encourage uniformity.
- *Providing activities that are open-ended.* It is the process of self-initiated creation that is rich and nourishing, not that of receiving and executing instructions.
- *Emphasizing the process, not the product.* A child who has made a painting that is not beautiful in a traditional sense is not unartistic and has accomplished much: he/she has enjoyed the sensation of moving paint across a surface and has learned about how colors mix, while developing fine motor skills.
- *Being as open and curious as the children are.* Don't feel that you have to be an "artist" to enjoy making art. Children are not concerned with how talented you are; rather, they are encouraged by your enthusiasm and participation.

Barriers to the Arts in Early Education

Despite the compelling evidence for the significance of the arts, many barriers exist that have limited the role of the arts in education. These include: a shift towards academic standards as evidence of school readiness, lack of arts-oriented professional development for educators, conflicts about appropriate program focus, and, finally, funding. When budgets are tight, arts programs and supplies are often cut first.

In schools today, even at the early childhood level, the emphasis continues to shift towards a narrow definition of school readiness. This trend leaves less time for children to engage in the arts.

Art is often left to educators who may not be prepared or comfortable with their own creativity and playfulness. In many cases, supplies, equipment, and adequate space are not provided for arts experiences. Professional development opportunities to support educators are critical to an arts-infused curriculum.

Finally, early education, except for certain low-income programs, is considered a private service and receives little or no federal funding. While the importance of early childhood arts education has received greater attention in recent years, the majority of funding and programming is directed to grades K-12, with early childhood centers being largely underserved. Arts education should not be considered a frill, but rather a necessity.

References

Arts Education Partnership. (1998). *Young children and the arts: Making creative connections. A report of the Task Force on Children's Learning and the Arts: Birth to Eight.* Washington, DC: Author.

Eisner, E. (2002). *The arts and the creation of mind.* New Haven and London: Yale University Press.

Isenberg, J. P., & Jalongo, M. R. (1966). *Creative expression and play in the early childhood curriculum* (2nd ed.). Upper Saddle River, NJ: Merrill/Prentice Hall.

Jensen, E. (1998). *Teaching with the brain in mind.* Alexandria, VA: Association for Supervision and Curriculum Development.

Murfee, E. (1995). *Eloquent evidence: Arts at the core of learning.* Washington, DC: National Assembly of State Arts Agencies.

Newberger, J. J. (1997). New brain development research—A wonderful window of opportunity to build public support for early childhood education! *Young Children, 52*(4), 4-9.

Shore, R. (1997). *Rethinking the brain: New insights into early development.* New York: Families and Work Institute.

PLAY AND THE CHILD WITH DISABILITIES
Sonia Mastrangelo & Isabel Killoran

CHAPTER 7

I tried to teach my child from books,
He gave me only puzzled looks.
I tried to teach my child with words,
They passed him by, often unheard.
Despairingly I turned aside,
"How shall I teach this child?" I cried.
Into my hand he put the key:
"Come," he said, "play with me."
—Author Unknown

Play is a complex phenomenon that occurs naturally for most children. They move through the various stages of play development and are able to add complexity, imagination, and creativity to their thought processes and actions. Many believe play is pivotal to young children's cognitive, motor, and social development. For example, Elkonin (1977, 1978) identifies four ways that play influences child development: 1) it affects the child's motivation, 2) it facilitates cognitive decentering, 3) it advances the development of mental representations, and 4) it fosters the development of deliberate behaviors, or motor and mental voluntary actions (as cited in Bodrova & Leong, 2004). However, for many children with disabilities, the various stages of play may never truly develop or they may occur in a fragmented fashion. Difficulties in motor planning, expressive and receptive communication, imitation, and fine and gross motor movements are just some of the many obstacles some children with disabilities encounter during play.

This chapter includes a review of the current literature on play for children with disabilities, the challenges associated with play as it pertains to this population, play and inclusion (including play strategies, adaptations, accommodations, and modifications), developing play goals for the Individual Education Plan (IEP), and assessing the play behaviors of exceptional children.

Play and the Child With Disabilities: What Does the Literature Tell Us?

Children with disabilities are included less often in interactive play than their peers without disabilities. Although degrees of social separation do seem to vary with severity of disability, even children with mild disabilities are less accepted as playmates than children without disabilities (Diamond & Stacey, 2000). Also, the play of children with disabilities differs considerably from that of their typically developing peers. For example, play repertoires are reported to be more limited and play incidences less frequent in children with developmental disabilities. The limitations of play may be even more pronounced for children with motor disabilities. The amount of actual time that children with motor disabilities spend in play is short and primarily solitary in nature (Kaplan-Sanoff, Brewster, Stillwell, & Bergen, 1988, p. 5). The play of children with multiple disabilities is often sedentary and passive, involves limited materials, and over-emphasizes either large- or small-motor actions; in addition, their parents' expectations generally are either too high or too low. Consequently, these children experience play deprivation, which may be related to the type and severity of their disability (Kaplan-Sanoff et al., 1988). In addition to facing physical and cognitive barriers, many children cannot initiate play or maintain an activity with peers. Children with disabilities need to learn how to become "intentional communicators," which will allow them to engage in more complicated social interactions (McCathren & Watson, 2001, p. 25).

Toys have the potential to strengthen the play experiences of children with disabilities. However, Bradley (1985) notes that they can become an obstacle to learning rather than a facilitator of the process, since the difficulty of using many toys can cause frustration. Parents of children with disabilities also may unknowingly promote play deficits and feelings of incompetence among their children. According to Hanzlik (1989), mothers of children with disabilities play with them less and are more controlling than are mothers of typically developing children. Interactions between mothers and their infants with disabilities indicate that infants provide fewer cues and initiate interaction less frequently than do their typically developing peers. These mothers often dominate the initiations. However, as the child grows older, parents have been noted to withdraw and spend less time playing. According to Jackson, Robey, Watjus, and Chadwick (1991), parents of young children with disabilities experience a shift in their role of parent as play partner to one of medical overseer/coordinator. "Spontaneous interactions become inhibited by the parent's anxiety over the medical condition of their child as well as by the reduced level of responsiveness that many children with disabilities exhibit" (Mistrett, Lane, & Goetz, 2000, p. 6).

Children with disabilities may experience a conflict between their internal drive to play and their inability to access play. Quite often, children with disabilities begin to develop learned helplessness because of their inability to control or communicate with the environment (Mistrett et al., 2000, p. 6). Children have a drive to interact with the physical and social world; when children with disabilities feel incompetent, they begin to learn (and believe) that they *cannot* do or *cannot* achieve. This learned helplessness exacerbates the problem, because many adults believe it, too, and reinforce it; thus, the children's self-esteem decreases.

The benefits of play on the development of cognitive, social-emotional, communication-language, and sensorimotor domains are well-recognized in the literature. However, for children with disabilities, their education programs are often made up of strict medical, academic, and therapeutic interventions to compensate for so-called "deficits." For them, the academic focus is on skill development, and play is regularly used as a reward *after* the child has worked through various program areas. As a result, play is often excluded in the programming for children with disabilities and is not considered "important" enough to include on the IEP. In their discussion of factors limiting the possibilities for play, Anderson, Hinojosa, and Strauch (1987) state that "when play is limited by both internal (individual) and external (environmental) factors, the ability to learn and develop the skills and attitudes associated with play is also limited" (as cited in Mistrett, Lane, & Goetz, 2000, p. 10). The goal for both teachers and parents is to find ways to incorporate play into day-to-day experiences. Furthermore, they need to build on the child's existing play abilities and consider the limitations of the disability by providing the necessary accommodations, adaptations, and modifications to teaching and to the environment.

Play Strategies and Interventions:
Creating Possibilities Among the Challenges

One of the greatest challenges for parents and educators is to overcome the need to direct a child's play. Choice and control are essential in play, because they give children a sense of ownership, allow risk taking, and promote creativity, appreciation, and confidence. Educators face a difficult situation when they must decide either to stand back and be an observer or jump in to extend and enrich children's play and development. According to Greenspan and Wieder (1998), the four goals of play include: encouraging attention and intimacy, promoting two-way communication, encouraging the expression and use of feelings/ideas, and logical thought.

For many children with disabilities, mastering an emotional milestone often occurs during play. This could mean acquiring the ability to feel calm and focused. It's hard to start working on so basic a skill when your child is two, three, or even older. It is tempting to work instead on language skills, colour recognition, or some other age appropriate behaviour; but such an approach is not effective. (p. 125)

Greenspan and Wieder (1998) provide general guidelines for teachers and parents to follow when engaging a child with disabilities in play. These include: stay patient and relaxed, empathize with the child's emotional tone, be aware of your own feelings, monitor your tone of voice and gestures, follow the child's lead and interact, and tune into the child's multiple developmental levels (pp. 128-129). One of the most important guidelines—following the child's lead—requires the teacher or parent to look for ways to turn all child actions during play into interactions. This involves treating all behavior as purposeful and as an opportunity to build two-way communication (p. 128).

Spodek and Saracho (1998) suggest that preparation is the most powerful strategy a teacher can use. Without a teacher preparing the environment, the materials, and the peers, opportunities for play may not happen for children with disabilities. One also must prepare the child with a disability for the activity. In discussing a child who is blind, Orr (2003) identified four questions that need answering before the child can become fully functional: 1) Where am I? 2) Who am I with? 3) What's happening?, and 4) What is happening next? Answering these questions would benefit all children. By answering these questions proactively, transitions will be easier and resistance should be less frequent.

There is a strong belief among educators, particularly those in the traditional field of special education, that children with disabilities require more direct instruction than do their typically developing peers. Therefore, play is often regarded as an add-on to the program.

The value of play can be difficult to explain to those who adhere to more traditional methods of direct instruction. Even more difficult is trying to convince these proponents of direct teaching and drill on isolated skills that young children do not learn well this way. (Callas, Bruns-Mellinger, & King-Taylor, 1998, p. 21)

It is possible, however, to embed direct instruction into free play; although by doing so, some researchers would argue that it is no longer play. Smith, Warren, Yoder, and Feurer (2004) state that direct teaching strategies used with young children with disabilities during free play and snack is a sign of program quality. Teachers with higher levels of specialized training were more likely to implement these strategies during free play. Although positive reinforcement is often used to encourage positive interaction during free play, some research indicates that some children learn a task more quickly if you stop talking to them about it (Biederman, Davey, Ryder, & Franchi, 1994). Difficulties with language may prevent them from listening and doing simultaneously.

The Importance of Play for the Child With a Disability

Play naturally promotes language development. Whether it is the child just beginning to make sounds as she moves a car down a ramp or whether it is the child involved in an intricate drama where a doll has been injured, language is a valuable byproduct that emanates from all forms of symbolic and sociodramatic play.

The idea that play and language are interrelated is not surprising since both serve several joint functions in the young child's life: first, both involve a communicative function of sharing objects with others; and second, children use both play and language to experiment and thereby learn about symbolic transformations and various self-other relationships. Whereas play clearly precedes the advent of language, play is in one sense itself a form of language because it incorporates symbolic representation. Play has been regarded as instrumental in developing both the comprehension and production aspects of language. (Barnett, 1990, p. 142)

Piaget identified the representational function provided by play and suggested that play is facilitative of children's aural language comprehension. He noted that playing out a drama forces a child to do several things.

First, the child becomes actively involved in the experience—they are no longer just hearing words, they are recreating events. Second, in order to physically recreate the events, the child must create a mental representation of the events. Third, the child must engage in social interaction to coordinate his/her play, and this social interaction acts further to help the child create a mental representation of the event. (as cited in Barnett, 1990, p. 142)

Children who are nonverbal also reap these benefits. Through gestures, vocalizations, or augmentative and adaptive communication systems, they are able to interact reciprocally with their peers and their environment, which contributes to broader and more complex understandings.

Research suggests that "young children with disabilities may have less stimulating literacy environments at home and in preschool than children without disabilities" (Hanline, 2001, p. 14). Consequently, it is especially important that teachers provide play experiences that support emergent literacy. Play provides the opportunity to interact with books and print materials, to see other children and adults using print in functional ways, and to develop oral language and phonemic awareness skills. Play-based activities also allow children to develop and refine motor and visual skills and engage in symbolic thinking (Hanline, 2001).

Greenspan and Wieder (1998) have done extensive research with children who have autism spectrum disorder and report that early intervention, coupled with daily opportunities for symbolic play, helps the child move up the developmental ladder. Through idea-laden play and expanding use of words, the child begins to learn that symbols stand for things (e.g., the empty box in which he bathes his doll is a symbol for a bathtub; therefore, the word "bath" is a symbol for his activity in the tub). "Each symbol is an idea, an abstraction of the concrete thing, activity or emotion with which the child is concerned. As he/she experiments more and more with symbolic play and words, he/she becomes increasingly fluent in the world of ideas" (p. 83).

Play and Inclusion:
A Look at Adaptation and Accommodation

An occupational therapist recently observed a child with autism spectrum disorder in his regular grade 2 classroom as he picked up various objects, threw them up in the air, and watched them fall to the ground. The child's educational assistant was insistent that this behavior be extinguished because it was disruptive to the rest of the class; she also believed that the child was simply seeking negative attention. The assistant's strategy was to ignore the behavior or to place the child in a time-out every time he dropped objects. The occupational therapist quickly realized that the falling objects served as a visual stimulus for this child with autism. As the objects fell to the ground, the boy watched their trajectory using his peripheral vision. The occupational therapist quickly met with the special education team and provided the necessary strategies and interventions to facilitate the boy's need to track objects peripherally, while respecting the school's philosophy of inclusion. Her suggestions included: giving the child opportunities to throw objects in a turn-taking situation with other peers during appropriate times (such as physical education); providing frequent opportunities for visual stimulus, within the context of game-playing situations with peers (such as tracking an infra-red flashlight in a dark room with other students); and allowing the student to do some research on falling objects with peers, within the framework of the science curriculum (such as experiments on the speed of falling objects and determining which will fall to the ground first). In essence, the occupational therapist suggested accommodating the child's program in an effort to meet his sensory needs while keeping inclusion at the forefront. All of her suggestions could be facilitated through play.

Inclusion can play an important role in creating equitable play situations. Proponents of inclusion believe that it is vital to encourage social interactions between children with disabilities and their typical peers, and they cite research studies showing that inclusive programs promote such social interactions and lead to greater learning and social competence (see, for example, Brown & Bergen, 2002; Killoran, 2002). Students with disabilities in general education classes experience improved educational outcomes when compared with peers in special education classrooms (see, for example, Hunt, Farron-Davis, Beckstead, Curtis, & Goetz, 1994; Rea, McLaughlin, & Walther-Thomas, 2002).

According to Fromberg (2002), teachers must remain conscious of the principles that define play and must be sensitive to the choices made by children with disabilities. The teacher becomes a very important person in this equation of play and inclusion, since she has the power to break down the barriers facing children with disabilities (i.e., inadequate materials, lack of opportunities to play with peers, inaccessible toys in the environment, etc). Some of the ways to eliminate these barriers include providing environmental support; adapting materials; simplifying the play activity by reducing the number of steps; basing the activity on the child's preferences; and providing special equipment/assistive technology, adult support, peer support, and invisible support through naturally occurring events (Sandall, 2004, p. 44-45).

Fromberg (2002) outlines the following accommodations and adaptations in order to ensure successful play opportunities for children with disabilities in the inclusive classroom:

- *Motor Setting*: height equipment, clipboards with fasteners to hold down paper or board games, card stands, and textured materials
- *Materials*: fist-accessible hand-grips on housekeeping play materials, frames for holding blocks, left-handed and four-fingered scissors
- *Amount of Time Available for Participation*: stagger the time available for different children to engage in play
- *Clear Contrasts*: focus a single, clear figure against a familiar background, and provide an environment that is relatively free of unnecessary visual or auditory distractions
- *Pacing*: provide sufficient advance notice for closing down, cleanup, and transition to another activity; minimize and reduce the number of transitions during the day. (p. 127)

Adaptations, accommodations, and modifications are essential when developing play provisions for children of all abilities in the inclusive classroom.

Outdoor Play

For typically developing children, learning through outdoor play experiences comes easily and naturally. Conversely, children with disabilities may have quite a different experience when playing outdoors. Some children lack the concentration skills to sustain their play experience, or the mobility to use the apparatuses. For others, the inability to communicate may prevent them from initiating a play activity they otherwise may have enjoyed with a play partner. Teachers and parents must be cognizant of the potential for social isolation at the park or on the recess playground. Providing positive, inclusive outdoor experiences for children is vital to their social and emotional development, as well as cognitive development.

According to Flynn and Kieff (2002), all children should be able to have fun outside, participate in activities with each other, and achieve learning goals through accommodations and adaptations (p. 21). They suggest the following guidelines for implementing inclusive outdoor play experiences. Learning is a sensory activity, and so teachers must reflect on the quality and quantity of the multisensory activities available to children. A child who has compromised sensory input (such as blindness) may have an over-reliance on one or two senses during outdoor play. Teachers also must promote independence for all children by adapting equipment to ensure that children do not develop learned helplessness (for example, by adding golf tees to the hammer at the woodworking center so that the child with low muscle tone can hold it). Flynn and Kieff also provide an extensive table of possible adaptations and accommodations for children with specific disabilities.

Teachers should encourage the use of cooperative learning groups. In order to foster interaction among peers of all abilities, it is essential to group children so that reciprocal exchanges of communication can occur. This may include teaching students how to use picture symbols (e.g., PECS), allowing the child who is nonverbal to request specific items from other children while playing in the sandbox, for example. Bradley (1989) identifies four statements that a child must be able to communicate if she is to gain some control over her life: 1) stay with me, 2) leave me alone, 3) give me more of this activity, and 4) give me less of this activity (as cited in Orr, 2003). Being able to communicate these statements would facilitate positive interactions with a child's peers and adults.

Developing Play Goals for an Individual Education Plan

Because many parents (and teachers, for that matter) view play as an extra, they are not inclined to see the value of including it on the IEP. This is especially true as the child moves through the primary grades. Many think that an emphasis on play takes away from academic learning. Bodrova and Leong's (2001) research clearly shows the opposite to be true. Children who were in classrooms where teachers used Vygotskian strategies to enhance play and who spent almost half of their class time in play scored higher in literacy skills than did children in the control classrooms (p. 10).

Teachers are responsible for setting up the environment and choosing materials that circumvent barriers, for designing peer social situations, and for fostering the development of specific skills (Davis, Kilgo, & Gamel-McCormick, 1998). Positive peer interactions may not develop without specific interventions (Chandler, 1998). IEP play goals can cross various domains of the curriculum. These include behavioral development, social-emotional development, cognitive development, communication, organization, and motor development (see Table 1 for a list of possible goals that may be addressed during play experiences). We

Table 1
IEP Goals That Connect to Play Experiences

- Interact with peers of all abilities, interests, and talents
- Develop social/communication skills by providing peer play opportunities
- Develop turn-taking skills through play experiences
- Become an active participant during cooperative play time
- Sustain attention and concentration
- Develop initiative and risk-taking behaviors by spontaneously inviting peers to play
- Learn rules of safety during indoor and outdoor play
- Learn the concept of personal space during play interactions
- Develop self-confidence and self-esteem
- Use verbal expression in group play situations
- Develop expressive/receptive language skills through play
- Develop skills in written expression
- Develop creativity and curiosity
- Increase flexibility and adaptability during changes in play routines
- Develop independent thinking and problem-solving strategies
- Develop independent use of specialized equipment during play
- Develop life skills
- Develop play skills
- Develop self-advocacy
- Develop mobility skills (for a student with a motor disability)
- Develop orientation/mobility skills (for a student who is visually impaired or blind)
- Develop sight enhancement or sight substitution techniques (for a student who is visually impaired or blind)
- Develop choice-making skills
- Develop and/or continue to develop relationships and maintain friendships
- Improve eye/hand coordination
- Develop fine and gross motor skills.

Adapted from: Dufferin Peel Catholic District School Board (2004). *The IEP Engine.*

can take any one of the goals listed and develop learning expectations/skills, indicate the teaching strategies/accommodations, and list the assessment strategies for that particular goal. For example, the goal to develop social/communication skills for the student with autism spectrum disorder can be broken into sub-components.

Learning Expectations/Skills:
- Learn and generalize the rules of social interaction (e.g., reciprocity, turn taking, etc.)
- Understand the nonverbal social behavior of others
- Use appropriate nonverbal communication (i.e., eye gaze, facial expression, conventional gestures, volume, rate of speech, etc.)
- Maintain an acceptable social distance
- Be able to begin, maintain, and end a conversation
- Develop coping skills (i.e., regarding anxiety, frustration, etc.)
- Self-correct during conversations and also ask for clarification
- Minimize difficulties in topic management (i.e., topic shifting, preoccupation with one topic)
- Learn to initiate play with peers.

Teaching Strategies/Accommodations:
- Teach problem-solving/decision-making/conflict resolution skills
- Teach initiating techniques
- Use social stories, comic strip conversations, and scripts
- Use videos
- Use drama and role-play
- Use cooperative games
- Pair with student of similar interests
- Use inclusive strategies (e.g., circle of friends, peer mentors)
- Use inclusive language and encourage collaboration
- Invite participation in groups
- Teach perspective taking
- Provide a safe and accepting classroom and school environment.

Assessment Strategies:
- Track frequency of positive/negative interactions during play
- Anecdotal reports
- Student self-assessment
- Conference with students, parents, staff, agencies
- Record effectiveness of techniques used.

The play curriculum is filled with opportunities for children to develop skills in various areas. Aside from this, a child may be working on specific play expectations that may need to be modified from the grade level curriculum, depending on the child's individual needs. With adequate play provisions, children with disabilities can flourish socially, emotionally, and cognitively. Table 2 outlines a variety of approaches to play that foster development across domains (e.g., Embedded Learning Opportunities, Peer Interaction Play Center, Prelinguistic Milieu Teaching). When teachers learn to articulate on the IEP the endless possibilities for the development of skills through play, parents will be more inclined to accept and embrace a curriculum that is based on a child's developmental level and encompasses his/her interests and motivations.

Parents have the opportunity to foster development through play just as often, if not more often, than teachers do. Time at the park, play dates, family game time, and car games are just a few of the opportunities to make play a priority. Rough and tumble play is an integral part of a child's development and most children with disabilities benefit from it. Yet, quite naturally, parents, usually fathers, often do not engage in as much rough and tumble play with children with disabilities because of their medical concerns. Sonksen et al. (1984) describe the essential nature of rough and tumble play on the development of the vestibular system and the importance

Table 2

Approaches That Foster Play Interactions

Prelinguistic Milieu Teaching (PMT) (McCathren & Watson, 2001)

Goal: To teach children to become intentional communicators
To teach requesting and commenting to young children
To communicate more frequently and with greater clarity
To provide opportunities for adults to respond
To facilitate the use of vocalizations, coordinated attention, and gestures to establish joint attention

When and where: Naturalistic environments
Various activities
In response to child's interests and actions

Specific strategies that are used: Motor imitation
Vocal imitation
Vocal model
Descriptive talk
Prompting for eye contact
Linguistic mapping
Gesture model
Combinations of the above

For specific examples of strategies at use and the theory behind them, see McCathren, R. B., & Watson, A. L. (2001). Facilitating the development of intentional communication. In M. Ostrosky & S. Sandall (Eds.), *Teaching strategies: What to do to support young children's development. Young Exceptional Children, Monograph Series No. 3* (pp. 25-35). Longmont, CO: Sopris West.

Using AAC Systems With Peers (Garfinkle & Schwartz (2001)

Goal: To increase peer-directed communication
To increase social communication with peers

When and where: Whenever and wherever peers are together

Specific intervention:

Step 1: Make sure the child with the disability is a fluent and persistent user of the AAC system.

Step 2: Arrange a small group (3 to 5 children) environment so that children are responsible for distributing the materials needed to participate; make sure there are materials preferred by the child with the disability and make sure the child has materials needed to participate, but not her preferred materials, so that she must communicate to get them.

Step 3: Support by prompting peer-to-peer communication.

Step 4: Encourage generalization of the peer interaction skills across peers, materials, and environments.

For a full description, see Garfinkle, A. N., & Schwartz, I. S. (2001). "Hey! I'm talking to you": A naturalistic procedure to teach preschool children to use their AAC systems with peers. In M. Ostrosky & S. Sandall (Eds.), *Teaching strategies: What to do to support young children's development. Young Exceptional Children, Monograph Series No. 3* (pp. 47-57). Longmont, CO: Sopris West.

Table 2 (continued)

Prelinguistic Milieu Teaching (PMT) (McCathren & Watson, 2001)

Goal: To provide instruction through modeling, verbal prompting, and motor guidance
To learn more complex skills within the context of the general curriculum through fun and meaningful activities
To create more teachable moments

Where: Embed in ongoing activities (including play) in natural settings

Strategy:

Step 1: Using the IEP, identify a learning objective that can be addressed in the classroom, or modify a learning objective so that it can be embedded in multiple activities and routines.

Step 2: Identify opportunities that naturally occur or could be modified to address each objective.

Step 3: Determine what modifications are needed, whether instruction is needed, what your role is, how you will respond to the child when she completes the task, and how you will evaluate it.

For details on setting up matrices and procedures, see Horn, E., Lieber, J., Sandall, S., & Schwartz, I. (2001). Embedded learning opportunities as an instructional strategy for supporting children's learning in inclusive programs. In M. Ostrosky & S. Sandall (Eds.), *Teaching strategies: What to do to support young children's development. Young Exceptional Children, Monograph Series No. 3* (pp. 59-69). Longmont, CO: Sopris West.

Peer Interaction Play Center (PALS) (Chandler, 1998)

Goal: To foster positive peer interactions
To foster friendships

When/where: Once established, the PALS center becomes one of the options during free play

Strategy:

There are four variables to arrange: peers, adults, materials and toys, and activity structure

1. Children with social delays play with peers who have more age-appropriate skills; rotate peers
2. Adults prompt and reinforce positive peer interaction when necessary; fade when possible
3. Materials are limited in number and variety and promote social play
4. Adults provide initial structure by describing social and play goals and child roles.

For activities and materials that promote social interaction and for specific strategies with each variable, see Chandler, L. (1998). Promoting positive interaction between preschool age children during free play: The PALS Center. *Young Exceptional Children, 1*(3), 14-19.

Can-do Thinking (Hull, Venn, Lee, & Van Buren, 2000)

Goal: To plan for success
To focus on child's preferences
To identify the way the child typically functions
To embed intervention strategies in everyday routines and activities

Where: In any setting where a child with a disability is, but particularly in inclusive ones

Strategy:

Step 1: Identify what the child is interested in; identify preferences for materials, activities, peers.

Step 2: Complete a can-do chart documenting what the child does in various centers, activities.

Step 3: Complete an inventory of what the child can do (mobility, communication, intellectual growth, self care, socialization, play).

Step 4: Examine the learning environment, expectations, rules, and routines.

Step 5: Based on the IEP (if there is one), the child's can-do inventory, and the classroom's objectives, etc., identify what you want for the child—same behavior, learn a new behavior, increase complexity of a behavior.

Step 6: Create a responsive environment.

For a specific case example and more detail, see Hull, K., Venn, M., Lee, J., & Van Buren, M. (2000). Passports for learning in inclusive settings. In S. Sandall & M. Ostrosky (Eds.), *Natural environments and inclusion. Young Exceptional Children, Monograph Series 2* (pp. 69-77). Longmont, CO: Sopris West.

of including it in the play repertoire (as cited in Orr, 2003). Yack, Sutton, and Aquilla (1998) also include roughhousing as an important activity for children with proprioceptive dysfunction.

As mentioned above, the family is key to promoting play in a child's life. The Let's Play! Project uses play as an outcome for families and children with disabilities. It argues that assistive technology must go hand-in-hand with play strategies for all children with disabilities (Lane & Mistrett, 2002). These authors suggest that play becomes secondary for a child who has to focus on physical requirements, such as balance and posture, and that the focus needs to be put back on play. The rationale of the project addresses the foci of families, assistive technology, and play.

- If play is how all children grow, then children with disabilities need as much access to play as do children without disabilities.
- If families in early intervention believe in the value of play, then they will identify play as a desired outcome for their child and interventions will be provided.
- If play is supported with assistive technology, then children with disabilities will have more opportunities to play, and their families will find more enjoyment in these activities.
- If children have more opportunities to play, then their skills will develop in all domains.
- If the children's skills develop, then families and practitioners will value play, and children will be afforded more opportunities to play and be playful.

(Let's Play! Project Rationale. *From* Lane, S. J., & Mistrett, S. (2002). Let's play! Assistive technology interventions for play. *Young Exceptional Children, 5*(2), 19-27.)

Assessing Children's Play

The above section mentioned some of the ways to assess a child's skills during play. Teachers must remember to remain flexible and develop assessment strategies specific to the child and the play activity. Some methods include allowing oral presentation of learning, conferencing with the student, and breaking play activities into smaller chunks in order to assess them separately. One method to assess children's play involves using a chart with the various classroom centers listed. The chart also can include various play behaviors (e.g., specific IEP objectives) and provide room for the assessor to check off and comment on whether the child is demonstrating any of the behaviors at the specific centers (see Table 3 for an example). Teachers assess and evaluate a child with disabilities during play by listening to language; analyzing social behaviors within the activity; observing how the child selects, approaches, and completes play tasks; observing how the child interacts with other children; and observing how the child uses manipulatives (Barrett, Littleford, Valee, & Wannamaker, 2000). Continuous assessment of children's play allows the teacher to: 1) determine the child's current strengths, needs, and interests; 2) create appropriate curriculum expectations on the IEP; 3) adequately plan, implement, and revise the child's program; 4) pinpoint specific difficulties; and 5) inform parents, support personnel, and other teachers about the child's development.

Conclusion

Play can serve as an intrinsically motivating and driving force in the lives of children with disabilities. Many opportunities for play must be provided, both in the home and school environment, since it is through play experiences that children flourish and develop skills in the cognitive, social, emotional, and motor domains. Teachers and parents should provide opportunities for play that access different sensory modalities. Furthermore, teaching peers how to be effective play partners and how to communicate with a child with disabilities ensures mutual enjoyment in the play experience and optimal levels of reciprocity. Whether the goal is to have the child use objects constructively, engage in socio-dramatic play, play simple structured games with a partner, initiate cause-and-effect play, play games with simple rules, or turn-take with one play partner, play enables the child to learn about the world around him and to test ideas, ask questions, and discover answers. It is a critical contributor to the development of all children and needs to be incorporated at all levels of learning.

Table 3. Observed Play Behaviors at Various Centers

Student:_____ Date: _____	Purposeful exploration of materials/ toys (learns through trial/ error)	Sustains interest in play	Imitates play behaviors of play partner	Demon- strates prob- lem solving	Asks questions for clarification
Dress-Up/House					
Sand					
Water Table					
Playground					
Puppets					
Arts and Crafts					
Blocks/ Construction					

References

Anderson, J., Hinojosa, J., & Strauch, C. (1987). Integrating play in neurodevelopmental treatment. *American Journal of Occupational Therapy, 41*(7), 421-426.

Barnett, L. A. (1990). Developmental benefits of play for children. *Journal of Leisure Research, 22*(2), 138-153.

Barrett, J., Littleford, J., Valee, J., & Wannamaker, N. (2000). *Kindergarten years: Learning through play.* Toronto: Elementary Teachers' Federation of Ontario.

Biederman, G. B., Davey, V. A., Ryder, C., & Franchi, A. S. (1994). The negative effects of positive reinforcement in teaching children with developmental delay. *Exceptional Children, 60,* 458-465.

Bodrova, E., & Leong, D. J. (2001). *The Tools of the Mind Project: A case study of implementing the Vygotskian approach in American early childhood and primary classrooms.* Geneva, Switzerland: International Bureau of Edcucation, UNESCO.

Bodrova, E., & Leong, D. J. (2004). Chopsticks and counting chips: Do play and foundational skills need to compete for the teacher's attention in an early childhood classroom? *Spotlight on Young Children and Play.* Washington, DC: National Association for the Education of Young Children.

Bradley, R. H. (1985). Social-cognitive development and toys. *Topics in Early Childhood Special Education, 5*(3), 11-30.

Brown, M., & Bergen, D. (2002). Play and social interaction of children with disabilities at learning/activity centers in an inclusive preschool. *Journal of Research in Childhood Education, 17*(1), 26-37.

Callas, J., Bruns-Mellinger, M., & King-Taylor, M. (1998). Play. In E. A. Tertell, S. M. Klein, & J. L. Jewett (Eds.), *When teachers reflect: Journeys toward effective, inclusive practice* (pp. 1-36). Washington, DC: National Association for the Education of Young Children.

Chandler, L. (1998). Promoting positive interaction between preschool age children during free play: The PALS Center. *Young Exceptional Children, 1*(3), 14-19.

Davis, M. D., Kilgo, J. L., & Gamel-McCormick, M. (1998). *Young children with special needs: A developmentally appropriate approach.* Boston: Allyn and Bacon.

Diamond, K. E., & Stacey, S. (2000). The other children at preschool: Experiences of typically developing children in inclusive programs. In S. Sandall & M. Ostrosky (Eds.), *Natural environments and inclusion.* Young Exceptional Children, Monograph Series 2 (pp. 59-68). Longmont, CO: Sopris West.

Dufferin Peel Catholic District School Board. (2004). *The IEP Engine.* Mississauga, ON: Author.

Flynn, L., & Kieff, J. (2002). Including everyone in outdoor play. *Young Children, 57*(3), 20-26.

Fromberg, D. P. (2002). *Play and meaning in early childhood education.* Boston: Allyn & Bacon.

Garfinkle, A. N., & Schwartz, I. S. (2001). "Hey! I'm talking to you": A naturalistic procedure to teach preschool children to use their AAC systems with peers. In M. Ostrosky & S. Sandall (Eds.), *Teaching strategies: What to do to support young children's development* (pp. 47-57). Young Exceptional Children, Monograph Series No. 3. Longmont, CO: Sopris West.

Greenspan, S. I., & Wieder, S. (1998). *The child with special needs: Encouraging intellectual and emotional growth.* Reading, PA: Addison-Wesley.

Hanline, M. (2001). Supporting emergent literacy in play-based activities. *Young Exceptional Children, 4*(4), 10-15.

Hanzlik, J. R. (1989). The effect of intervention on the free-play experience for mothers and their infants with developmental delay and cerebral palsy. *Motor and Occupational Therapy in Pediatrics, 9*(2), 33-51.

Hatcher, B., & Pettey, K. (2004). Visible thought in dramatic play. *Young Children, 59*(6), 79-82.

Horn, E., Lieber, J., Sandall, S., & Schwartz, I. (2001). Embedded learning opportunities as an instructional strategy for supporting children's learning in inclusive programs. In M. Ostrosky & S. Sandall (Eds.), *Teaching strategies: What to do to support young children's development* (pp. 59-69). Young Exceptional Children, Monograph Series No. 3. Longmont, CO: Sopris West.

Hull, K., Venn, M., Lee, J., & Van Buren, M. (2000). Passports for learning in inclusive settings. In S. Sandall & M. Ostrosky (Eds.), *Natural environments and inclusion.* Young Exceptional Children, Monograph Series 2. (pp. 69-77). Longmont, CO: Sopris West.

Hunt, P., Farron-Davis, F., Beckstead, S., Curtis, D., & Goetz, L. (1994). Evaluating the effects of placement of students with severe disabilities in general education versus special classes. *Journal of the Association for Persons with Severe Handicaps, 19,* 200-214.

Jackson, S. C., Robey, L., Watjus, M., & Chadwick, E. (1991). Play for all children: The toy library solution. *Childhood Education, 68,* 27-31.

Kaplan-Sanoff, M., Brewster, A., Stillwell, J., & Bergen, D. (1988). In D. Bergen (Ed.), *Play as a medium for learning and development: A handbook of theory and practice* (pp. 137-161). Portsmouth, NH: Heinemann.

Killoran, I. (2002). A road less traveled: Creating a community where each belongs. *Childhood Education, 78,* 371-377.

Lane, S. J., & Mistrett, S. (2002). Let's play! Assistive technology interventions for play. *Young Exceptional Children, 5*(2), 19-27.

McCathren, R. B., & Watson, A. L. (2001). Facilitating the development of intentional communication. In M. Ostrosky & S. Sandall (Eds.), *Teaching strategies: What to do to support young children's development.* Young Exceptional Children, Monograph Series No. 3 (pp. 25-35). Longmont, CO: Sopris West.

Mistrett, S., Lane, S., & Goetz, A. (2000). *A professional's guide to assisting families in creating play environments for children with disabilities: Let's play! project.* Buffalo, NY: University at Buffalo Center for Assistive Technology.

Orr, R. (2003). *My right to play: A child with complex needs*. Debating Play Series. Philadelphia, PA: Open University Press.

Rea, P., McLaughlin, V., & Walther-Thomas, C. (2002). Outcomes for students with learning disabilities in inclusive and pullout programs. *Exceptional Children, 68*(2), 203-222.

Sandall, S. R. (2004). Play modifications for children with disabilities. In D. Koralek (Ed.), *Spotlight on young children and play* (pp. 44-45). Washington, DC: National Association for the Education of Young Children.

Smith, J., Warren, S. F., Yoder, P. J., & Feurer, I. (2004). Teachers' use of naturalistic communication intervention practices. *Journal of Early Intervention, 27*(1), 1-14.

Sonksen, P. M., Lewitt, S., & Kitzinger, M. (1984). Identification of constraints on motor development in young visually disabled children and principles of remediation. *Child Care Health Development, 10*, 273-286.

Spodek, B., & Saracho, O. N. (1998). The challenge of educational play. In D. Bergen (Ed), *Readings from . . . Play as a medium for learning and development* (pp. 11-28). Olney, MD: Association for Childhood Education International.

Yack, E., Sutton, S., & Aquilla, P. (1998). *Building bridges through sensory integration*. Toronto, ON: Print 3.

OUTDOOR PLAY

Kathleen Burriss

CHAPTER 8

"The outside has weather and life,
the vastness of the sky, the universe
in the petals of a flower."
—Greenman, 2003b, p. 75

There is a long-standing relationship between children's play and their development, whether it is cognitive (Beaty, 2002; Berk, 1994; Flavell, 1985; Frost, Wortham, & Reifel, 2001; Hughes, 1995); social/emotional (Damon, 1983; Garvey, 1977; Isenberg & Jalongo, 2001; Kostelnik, Stein, Whiren, & Soderman, 1993; Piaget, 1962; Piers, 1972; Saracho & Spodek, 1998; Smilansky, 1968; Smilansky & Shefatya, 1990); or physical (Frost, Brown, Sutterby, & Thornton, 2004; Kostelnik et al., 1993). Building on this historical relationship between play and growth, this chapter proposes that outdoor play further extends benefits for children's development in ways that are not possible in traditional indoor activities. If we facilitate and encourage learning and playing out-of-doors, we can break down traditional boundaries between disciplines, provide hands-on experiences, allow students with a variety of learning styles and backgrounds to achieve success, foster students' skills and abilities, and increase children's willingness to stay on-task and improve their performance (Smith-Walters, 2005). The weather, open space, and plant and animal life are not to be avoided as obstacles for learning, but are, in fact, the very reasons to go out-of-doors (Greenman, 2003b).

The time children spend out-of-doors is not to be used as a reward given once the "real work" of school is complete. Nor is outdoor play merely an opportunity for children to "run off" extra energy. Rather, children's outdoor play has both developmental and academic legitimacy (Frost et al., 2004; National Association for the Education of Young Children, 1998).

What Do We Know About the Out-of-Doors?

Urban, suburban, and rural environments provide children with almost unlimited possibilities for outdoor play. A playscape is any area in which children can use materials, test their physical and mental skills, and find fodder for their curiosity. Playscapes move from the simple to the complex and are defined more broadly than playgrounds. An outdoor learning environment is more than just the space and the equipment available. "How the space is used and the range of learning experiences [that exist] for children is the glue that holds effective outdoor learning together" (McGinnis, 2002, p. 28). In other words, when moving children to the out-of-doors, teachers are transitioning to a different classroom—the outdoor classroom.

Greenman (2003a) believes, "Both at home and in child care, children are losing time, space, and the variety of experience outdoors that has been integral to the development of humankind" (p. 40). Greenman is concerned that children are losing their "sense of habitat." He sees today's children being driven to their destinations and escorted by adults, thereby missing opportunities for experiences "along the way." That is, children have "lost their sense of journey" (p. 41). Researchers have documented this trend toward limiting children's unsupervised exploration and wandering (Frost et al., 2004). In the past, children entertained themselves by creating adventures in their neighborhoods. Outdoor activities offer physical and personal challenges. Interactions with objects and peers provide practice in mediation, compromise, and construction of meaning about the world and its people (Perry, 2003). Children use materials, people, and events differently when they are outdoors. As in the case of indoor play, outdoor play takes both free and guided forms.

Free Play

In both indoor and outdoor play, children initiate, maintain, and culminate free play opportunities. During free play, children establish the goal for their play and freely choose materials to use in a variety of ways. The main role of the adult in free play is to provide time, space, and materials, then step back and observe the children at play. For example, as children engage in group-dramatic or constructive play, they recruit, plan, and initiate commonly shared themes. Christie and Wardle (1992) caution that children may encounter several false starts as they plan for roles and use objects and designated play areas. Therefore, they need at least 30-50 minutes to develop play themes. Adults ensure quality play by providing this time and providing adequate space with a variety of materials. Through observation, adults may determine that some children need assistance and consequently offer other materials or direct intervention (Johnson, Christie, & Yawkey, 1987).

Free play includes water, sand, and dirt play; self-initiated games (running, ball toss, jump rope); pretend play (rocking boat, bear-in-cave, race car driver); and drawing, painting, or sculpting (in snow, mud, sand). When observing children's outdoor play, teachers aware of child development know what to look for and when to intervene. For example, a grassy knoll may invite children's rough and tumble (R&T) play. In R&T play, children run, chase, and wrestle with no intent to capture or injure their playmates.

The slapping and rolling in R&T play is not aggressive, but rather is socially driven (Reed & Brown, 2002).

. . . R&T is also a place for negotiation, problem solving, fulfilling their need to belong to a group, having intimate contact with friends, experiencing friendly competition, and developing a sense of community somewhere between the warmth and closeness of family and the isolation and indifference of the adult masculine world. (p. 113)

In other words, as a free and playful expression of caring, the benefits of R&T for children outweigh the low risk of injury (Reed & Brown, 2002). With insight into such expressions of care and creativity by children, teachers do not interfere with free play.

Guided Play

In guided play, adults structure activities within a theme of study. Children's choices are purposefully integrated into curriculum objectives. As with indoor activities, outdoor centers/stations and activities relate to and support the theme of study by including academic objectives and state standards. "A learning center guides children's learning through play with its available materials, objects, and space; what children naturally enjoy doing with those materials; and the shared history of play in that area" (Perry, 2003, p. 27). For example, within a theme study of "Neighborhood Life," birdbaths and feeders serve as observational areas; art activities include outdoor sketches and paintings of animals and their habitats; constructive and thematic role-play replicate different animal homes; and documentation can be done for animal tracks and activity. Guided play does not negate children's free play. Rather, guided play is done in addition to free play, and so it enriches children's free expression.

What Does the Outdoor Classroom Look Like?

In order to promote quality outdoor learning and play, Perry (2003) suggests that playscapes be mapped out as carefully as indoor centers. It is important to designate particular areas for different types of play. Both natural (trees, water, sand) and man-made (benches, stages, toys) materials can be made available to children. In addition to these objects, children also need supportive adults. Finally, the outdoor classroom includes both passive (observation activities involving binoculars, telescopes, periscopes) and active (constructive play with blocks, sand, or wood, etc.) experiences (McGinnis, 2002).

Children use materials differently when outdoors, building on the natural resources of water, rocks, and trees. Picnic tables, benches, and stages can be added. Such areas provide children with a gathering place. According to Perry (2003), play yards with defined and protected places for small groups of children support their complex thinking and communication.

With community assistance and not much space or money, more complex playscapes can be constructed. Butterfly gardens, vegetable stations, and tree planting can provide quality play for children. Bird baths, animal feeders, and habitats provide a rich environmental backdrop for children's outdoor learning and play.

Sound can serve as a subtle background. Rustling leaves, blowing trees, and differently sized chimes (made from a variety of materials, such as metal, wood, and ceramic) all can enrich the playscape (Keeler, 2003). Keeler adds that including bells, chimes, and rattles contributes to children's outdoor play experiences. Other options include providing children with drums or xylophones.

More elaborate sites, such as ponds, wetlands, and nature trails, also can be used for outdoor areas: "The trend is to choose more ecologically valuable projects rather than beautification ones" (Rivkin, 1997, p. 64). In this way, schools create areas that attract wildlife and preserve local ecosystems (Pfouts & Schultz, 2003). Protecting the natural landscape provides for additional learning opportunities for children and further highlights the relationship between indoor and outdoor learning.

McGinnis (2002) cautions that making a smooth transition from the indoor to the outdoor classroom is important. She suggests using a transitional area, informing children at least 15 minutes prior to moving to the outdoor classroom, and providing them with five-minute reminders. Children may complete their indoor tasks or choose to take their activity out-of-doors. Portable tables and chairs facilitate an effective transition (McGinnis, 2002).

What Happens Out-of-Doors?

The key to effective outdoor learning is the ability of teachers to be aware of and plan for different outdoor activities. While still indoors, children research, discuss, and prepare for the outdoor experience. The outdoor classroom serves as a resource for relevant fieldwork. Different from the traditional field trip, fieldwork refers to children using observation, experimentation, and play to gather information about the real world. As they pursue fieldwork, children can collect information through rubbings, sketches, journals, learning logs, video or tape recordings, and photographs. After collecting the information, children demonstrate their newfound learning through narratives, graphs, charts, diagrams, and role-play (Chard, 1998). These types of outdoor activities are appropriate for all ages.

For younger ages, prop boxes or play crates connect the children's individual interests from the indoor to the outdoor classroom (McGinnis, 2002).

Prop boxes are containers for loose parts that are organized to offer a specific play theme such as dress-up, water play, sand play, or blocks and animals; a bubble crate, a digging and garden crate, or a boot and funshoe crate could be made. (p. 28)

When children go out-of-doors, they experience learning in ways not possible in traditional indoor settings.

What About Children With Special Needs?

Children with a variety of special needs also appreciate the social, emotional, cognitive, and physical possibilities found out-of-doors that are not available in the traditional indoor classroom. The spaciousness of the outdoor classroom enhances all children's sense of freedom (Flynn & Kieff, 2002). Although typically developing children may engage in outdoor play naturally, children with special needs may have difficulty initiating and sustaining such interactions. They also may process information more slowly and have communication difficulties. Despite the unique sensorial opportunities possible outdoors, children with special needs may still be isolated. Therefore, teachers should make themselves available to actively support inclusive play and promote independence for all children. Outdoor play builds on the strengths of children with special needs, just as it does for typically developing children. Children are better able to realize their potential outdoors if teachers check with parents in determining safety parameters and are subtle, not overt, in their supervision. The supportive community that exists indoors can be easily transferred to the outdoor classroom (Flynn & Kieff, 2002).

What About Playgrounds?

The quality of children's outdoor experience is defined by their playscape. Often, these arenas for play are referred to as playgrounds. "A playground should be like a small-scale replica of the world, with as many as possible of the sensory experiences to be found in the world included in it" (Johnson, Christie, & Yawkey, 1987, p. 205). However, Frost et al. (2004) caution that while many experts may be involved in the design of playgrounds, an understanding of children's development and play is frequently lacking. Instead, playgrounds are designed with respect to the budget, equipment choice, and adult preferences. Typically, there are three types of playgrounds: traditional, creative/contemporary, and adventure (Greenman, 2003b; Johnson, Christie, & Yawkey, 1987).

The traditional type is the playground most commonly observed in elementary schools. It is associated with large, immovable steel equipment (swings, slides, climbing bars, seesaws, and merry-go-rounds). Its primary function is to help children develop gross motor skills through exercise (Frost, 1992). Because it is difficult for children to change such traditional settings, their choices for play are limited. Greenman (2003b) suggests that because creative

Outdoor fieldwork provides children unique opportunities to observe, collect, and represent their world, even while using a pretend camera to take pictures of real airplanes.

Outdoor games with rules provide children opportunities to collaborate. Children learn that both winning and losing are part of the real world.

The out-of-doors provides sensorial learning not possible in the traditional indoor setting.

Through modeling, adults support children's understanding of the outdoor world and its people. Children increase their vocabulary, extend concepts, and learn to problem solve.

Children interact with others and share materials in ways unique to the out-of-doors.

and social play are restricted, children often initiate alternative uses of equipment (jumping off slides, swinging together, walking up the down-slide). Unfortunately, these alternative uses add elements of risk, which are compounded with the motion and varied heights of equipment, inadequate impact-cushion surfaces, and lack of supervision (Frost et al., 2004; Greenman, 2003b). Consequently, the traditional playground is associated with low usage, low-level play, and a high rate of injuries (Johnson, Christie, & Yawkey, 1987).

The creative or contemporary playground is designed to provide children with a varied and stimulating environment for play. The equipment is primarily wooden with some metal fixtures, and offers platforms, enclosed areas, pulleys, tree swings, tunnels, balance beams, and suspension bridges. Unlike the spread-out and isolated nature of the traditional playground, the creative playground is centrally located and connected. The surfaces are varied, including hard (concrete, asphalt) and soft (sand, wood chips, and grass). In this way, children can use wheeled toys, have safe surfaces around climbing equipment, and sit or run on the grass. Through the efforts of community volunteers, the creative/contemporary playground is often built with a regard for the natural landscape. Rarely, however, do creative/contemporary playgrounds provide for loose parts (Greenman, 2003b).

The third playground type, adventure playground, is sometimes referred to as a "junk" playground because the equipment is made up of discarded materials. Aside from the storage shed or clubhouse, all other materials are temporary. Wood, cables, rope, lumber, crates, and tires allow children to build, demolish, and rebuild. Loose parts are emphasized and nothing is permanent. This continual evolution of the adventure playground accounts for its popularity and success with children. Hammers and nails are available. Gardens and animal habitats are also included in the adventure playground. Finally, the safety record of the adventure playground is much higher, as constant supervision by an adult, referred to as the "play leader," is incorporated (Greenman, 2003b). However, with restricted space, diminished funds, and limited understanding of developmentally appropriate playscapes, what is the future for children's outdoor learning and play?

Where To Begin?

Outdoor environments that utilize natural features of the landscape and provide children with a variety of play (exercise, dramatic and constructive, and games with rules) maximize quality play and learning experiences (Isenberg & Jalongo, 2001; Rivkin, 1995). Greenman (2003a) conceives of a playscape where children can be children by placing the emphasis on the landscape, loose parts, and the thoughtful use of equipment. He suggests that budgets should reflect an understanding of child development by determining how children's needs can be met within particular developmental stages. "A good outdoor environment, even a very small one, might be one part traditional playground, one part vacant lot, one part outdoor classroom, one part back yard, and one part natural park" (p. 42). In other words, in creating quality playscapes, teachers must be aware of the relationship across children, learning, and child development.

Begin with a simple natural setting; across time, add other natural and man-made resources. The outdoor playscape does not have to be large. However, prepare for the area to evolve with time and planning. Most important, build the outdoor experience into the daily schedule. Community businesses and parents may be willing to assist with funding and construction. Try to secure funding from grants as well. Plan for a playscape that can be well-maintained.

What About the Future?

In her fictional story *The Giver* (1993), Lois Lowry describes a community in which the people create a world of sameness for convenience. No longer do they struggle with climate or landscape. As they give up the inherent problems of weather and terrain, however, the characters also lose their sense of independence, motivation, and exploration. Greenman (2003a) asks, "How do we become wise or spiritual without understanding our ecosystem and our place in it?" (p. 40). The outdoors offers children unique challenges to problem solve, negotiate, and communicate. In this hurried society, however, children's after-school schedules leave little or no time for outdoor play. When is the learning about and appreciation for the outdoors to occur?

A regard for the outdoors evolves from consistent interaction. This cannot be accomplished in a two-week summer vacation. Although located outside, theme and amusement parks do not constitute genuine interaction with the out-of-doors. Finally, any engagement with the out-of-doors must include appropriate regard for animal, fish, and bird life. With limited schedules, how do teachers and parents plan for quality outdoor time? Sometimes, the answers most desired are the simplest to make happen. Begin with one step, then another, and venture with a walk in the outdoor classroom; look, listen, smell, and appreciate.

References

Beaty, J. (2002). *Observing development of the young child* (5th ed.). New York: Prentice Hall.

Berk, L. (1994). Vygotsky's theory: The importance of make-believe play. *Young Children, 50*(1), 30-39.

Chard, S. C. (1998). *The project approach: Managing successful projects.* New York: Scholastic.

Christie, J., & Wardle, F. (1992). How much time is needed for play? *Young Children, 47*(3), 28-32.

Damon, W. (1983). *Social and personality development.* New York: W.W. Norton Company.

Flavell, J. (1985). *Cognitive development* (2nd ed.). Englewood Cliffs, NJ: Prentice Hall.

Flynn, L., & Keiff, J. (2002). Including everyone in outdoor play. *Young Children, 57,* 20-26.

Frost, J. L. (1992). *Play and playscapes.* New York: Delmar Publishers.

Frost, J., Wortham, S., & Reifel, S. (2001). *Play and child development.* New York: Prentice Hall.

Frost, J. L., Brown, P. S., Sutterby, J. A., & Thornton, C. D. (2004). *The developmental benefits of playgrounds.* Olney, MD: Association for Childhood Education International.

Garvey, C. (1977). *Play.* Cambridge, MA: Harvard University Press.

Greenman, J. (2003a). Are we losing ground? *Child Care Information Exchange,* March(150), 40-42.

Greenman, J. (2003b). Making outdoor learning possible. *Child Care Information Exchange,* May(151), 75-80.

Hughes, F. (1995). *Children, play, and development.* Boston: Allyn and Bacon.

Isenberg, J. P., & Jalongo M. R. (2001). *Creative expression in play in early childhood.* New York: Prentice Hall.

Johnson, J. E., Christie, J. F., Yawkey, T. D. (1987). *Play*

and early childhood development. Glenview, IL: Scott Foresman and Company.

Keeler, R. (2003, March). Designing and creating natural play environments for young children. *Child Care Information Exchange,* 43-45.

Kostelnik, M., Stein, L. C., Whiren, A. P., & Soderman, A. K. (1993). *Guiding children's social development.* Albany, NY: Delmar Publishers.

Lowry, L. (1993). *The giver.* New York: Bantam Doubleday Dell Publishing

McGinnis, J. R. (2002). Enriching the outdoor environment. *Young Children, 57,* 28-30.

National Association for the Education of Young Children. (1998). *Early years are learning years: The value of school recess and outdoor play.* Retrieved December 30, 2005, from www.naeyc.org/resources/eyly/1998/08.htm

Perry, J. P. (2003,). Making sense of pretend outdoor play. *Young Children, 58,* 26-30.

Pfouts, B., & Schultz, R. A. (2003). The benefits of outdoor learning centers for young gifted learners. *Gifted Child Today, 26*(1), 56-63.

Piaget, J. (1962). *Play, dreams and imitation in childhood.* New York: W.W. Norton & Company.

Piers, M. (Ed.). (1972). *Play and development.* New York: W.W. Norton & Company.

Reed, T., & Brown, M. (2002). The expression of care in the rough and tumble play of boys. *Journal of Research in Childhood Education, 15,* 104-111.

Rivkin, M. (1997). The schoolyard habitats movement: What it is and why children need it. *Early Childhood Education Journal, 25*(1), 61-66.

Saracho, O., & Spodek, B. (1998). *Multiple perspectives on play in early childhood education.* Albany, NY: State University of New York Press.

Smilansky, S. (1968). *The effects of sociodramatic play on disadvantaged preschool children*. New York: John Wiley & Sons.

Smilansky, S., & Shefatya, L. (1990). *Facilitating play: A medium for promoting cognitive, socio-emotional and academic development in young children*. Cambridge, MA: Psychosocial & Educational Publications.

Smith-Walters, C. (2005). The out-of-doors classroom: What is it? In K. G. Burriss & B. Foulks-Boyd (Eds.), *Outdoor learning & play: 8-12 years* (pp. 87-93). Olney, MD: Association for Childhood Education International.

*"Play needs to be cherished and encouraged,
for in their free play children reveal
their future minds." ~Friedrich Froebel (1887)*

Sadly, a common perception among parents, the general public, teachers, and administrators is that play is a fun, but aimless, activity. They often view play as a nice reward for children after they spend time engaged in more serious learning tasks (Henniger, 2005). Some traditional teachers consider play to be a waste of time with few benefits. These teachers are quick to ban play from their curriculum in order to focus more on drill-and-practice skills (DeVries, Zan, Hildebrandt, Edmiaston, & Sales, 2002). What are the benefits of play? Should play be purposefully planned for inclusion in the early childhood curriculum? Through the authors' contributions and perspectives on the importance of childhood play and our unified efforts, we collectively reach consensus that "To play or not to play: Is it really a question?" can be answered with a resounding "YES!" This book provides the reader with a solid and foundational understanding of the many benefits of play and makes a strong, undeniable case that play should be an integral component of curricular planning for young children.

To emphasize the benefits of play on the developing brain, in Chapter 1, Bergen presents the role of play in brain development, based on scientifically based investigations of brain activity. For example, play may exercise the frontal lobe of the brain, which has the capacity for critical thinking and problem solving. Children's play experiences in their early years have a profound impact on the structure and performance of their brains. In addition, the play choices that children make enhance synaptic growth, thus enriching the developing brain.

With the increased mobility of our global world, today's early childhood classrooms have become culturally and linguistically diverse. In Chapter 2, Szecsi and Giambo purport that early childhood educators should celebrate and build on this diversity among their students by creating a culturally responsive curriculum that offers playful experiences within cultural contexts of play. International examples are presented that provide awareness of culturally specific play experiences, promote first- and second-language learning, and encourage children to feel included and appreciated.

Because of the strong emphasis placed on academics in schools today and societal trends undermining childhood, there is evidence that imaginative, child-powered play is disappearing. This is a truly disturbing phenomenon. In Chapter 3, Dettore proposes several reasons why play is being challenged. For example, television and computers are replacing creative and imaginative play. More emphasis is being placed on standardized tests and less on creativity. Liability and safety issues and the demise of suitable playgrounds and green spaces prevent children from freely exploring nature. Additionally, children are being pressured to excel at the expense of enjoying and celebrating the joys of childhood.

As early childhood education moves front and center in the public policy debate, more attention is being paid to early literacy. Recognizing this focal point, toy manufacturers and software companies have developed toys and games designed for children to practice their emergent literacy skills, albeit artificially. In Chapter 4, Ferguson presents research that describes reading as a social process and sociodramatic play centers as natural settings for children to practice and explore their emergent literacy skills.

Both locally and globally, the ways of understanding and living in the world—including the issues of difference, identity, culture, and diversity—are big challenges for young children. In shaping children's cultural, social, and gender identities, the media, school cultures, and meaningful adults play decisive roles. In Chapter 5, McNulty asserts that play is essential in developing cultural identity and in satisfying children's curiosity about race and gender. Through the expansion of cognitive abilities, physical development, and conciliation of peer relations, play assumes a critical stance in influencing social and gender roles.

Despite compelling evidence that early arts experiences have an impact on all aspects of a child's learning and development, there exist many barriers to early or sustained arts experiences in early education. In Chapter 6, Booth, Ehrlich, and Deasy present convincing evidence that the arts are a natural way to support young children's growth across all developmental domains. The arts provide children with unrestricted opportunities to develop and strengthen imagination and critical thinking and to refine cognitive and creative skills.

Play is a complex and engaging phenomenon for most children, "yet its value seems to have eluded many educators of young children with disabilities, as well as their parents" (Jackson, Robey, Watjus, & Chadwick, 1991, p. 27). In Chapter 7, Mastrangelo and Killoran assert that one of the greatest challenges for educators and parents of children with disabilities is to overcome the need to direct a child's play. Allowing children with disabilities to have choice and control is essential in play because it provides them with a sense of ownership, encourages risk-taking, and promotes creativity and competence. Unfortunately, children with disabilities are less accepted by playmates; thus, they experience feelings of incompetence and play deprivation. Because of the focus on academics, play often is not considered to be important enough to include on the child's Individual Education Plan (IEP). The authors clearly present the benefits of play for children with disabilities as well as specific guidelines on how to incorporate play into an IEP.

With renewed emphasis on academics and recent trends toward adults structuring children's time, occasions for exploration are being limited. In Chapter 8, Burriss contends that the physical challenges offered by outdoor activities promote interactions with objects and peers that provide practice in mediation, compromise, and construction of meaning about the world and its people. These types of experiences in the outdoors give legitimacy to having both developmental and academic growth.

In conclusion, the contributors in this book strongly assert that play is an important vehicle for optimal child development. It has becoming increasingly clear, through research on the brain, that children need play. Further investigative studies support the power of play in honing the skills that children need to develop into functioning, productive adults. These skills include literacy, mathematical reasoning, creativity, problem solving and social skills. Today, children have so little time for unstructured play. The precious time they do have is being consumed by academic rigor, busy schedules, television, computers, and extracurricular activities. Finally, a new report from the American Academy of Pediatrics (AAP) affirms that free and unstructured play is healthy and, in fact, essential for helping children reach important social, emotional, and cognitive developmental milestones, as well as enabling them to manage stress and become resilient. When we consider all of these findings, does it leave us with any other answer to the query "to play or not to play"? The answer is clearly that children need to play. With this question answered, we wholeheartedly support Isenberg's and Quisenberry's (2002) proclamation that "the time has come to advocate strongly in support of play for *all* children" (p. 33).

—*Christine Jeandheur Ferguson & Ernest Dettore, Jr.*

References

Association for Childhood Education International/ Isenberg, J. P., & Quisenberry, N. (2002). Play: Essential for all children. A position paper. *Childhood Education, 79*, 33-39.

DeVries, R., Zan, B., Hildebrandt, C., Edmiaston, R., & Sales, C. (2002). *Developing constructivist early childhood curriculum.* New York: Teachers College Press.

Froebel, F. (1887). *The education of man.* New York: Appleton.

Henniger, M. L. (2005). Play in childhood (3rd ed.). In M. L. Henniger (Ed.), *Teaching young children: An introduction* (pp. 114-139). Upper Saddle River, NJ: Pearson.

Jackson, S. C., Robey, L., Watjus, M., & Chadwick, E. (1991). Play for ALL children: The toy library solution. *Childhood Education, 68*, 27-31.

Christine Jeandheur Ferguson is an Associate Professor in the Richard W. Riley College of Education at Winthrop University, Rock Hill, South Carolina. She supervises and instructs teacher candidates in early childhood field placements, early childhood mathematics methods, and child development. She also teaches early childhood graduate courses in curriculum and instruction. Christine is an active member of several state, national, and international organizations and currently serves as Chair of Student Groups for the South Carolina Early Childhood Association. Her research interests include children's literacy development through play, home/school literacy connections, teacher preparation, and technology infusion into teaching. As a former early childhood educator for 14 years, her experiences include teaching preschool, kindergarten, and special education.

Ernest Dettore, Jr. is a Technical Assistance Consultant for the Keystone STARS Quality Initiative at the University of Pittsburgh's Office of Child Development. He is also a PQAS-Certified Early Child Education Trainer for The Pennsylvania Early Learning Keys to Quality. Most recently, he has functioned as the Co-Director of the Early Childhood Initiative Demonstration Project at the University of Pittsburgh's Office of Child Development and as the Coordinator of Early Childhood Education Programs at Duquesne University. In his 33 years of experience in the field of early childhood care and education, Ernie has served as a university professor, a model instructor in a university lab school, an owner/operator of a child development center, a coordinator with Head Start, and as a teacher in a child development center. Ernie is certified in Early Child Education, has a Certificate in Child Care/Development, and holds a Doctorate in Early Childhood Education in Instruction and Learning from the University of Pittsburgh.

Doris Bergen is Professor of Educational Psychology at Miami University, Oxford, Ohio, and co-director of Miami University's Center for Human Development, Learning, and Technology. She teaches a range of courses related to learning, human development, assessment, and educational psychology. Her research interests have focused on cross-cultural programs for young children, play and humor in early and middle childhood, effects of technology-enhanced toys, adult memories of childhood play, social interactions of children with special needs, effects of early phonological awareness levels on later reading, and gifted children's humor development. She has published extensively, including the ACEI publication *Brain Research and Childhood Education*. She also served for 4 years as editor of ACEI's *Journal of Research in Childhood Education*.

Howard Booth has worked in the areas of early childhood education, the arts, and business for over 30 years. Howard has a BFA from Carnegie Mellon and an MBA from Duquesne University. His experience as an educator at Shady Lane, an early childhood center in Pittsburgh, Pennsylvania, with an arts-focused program model, ranged from teaching to serving as the Executive Director. He has also taught early education courses at the University of Pittsburgh. As a professional artist, he understands the connections between art and play(fulness) as well as the need for a sustainable business model.

Kathleen G. Burriss is a Professor in the Department of Elementary and Special Education at Middle Tennessee State University. Her research interests include play and outdoor learning. Publications include two ACEI books: *It's Elementary* and *Outdoor Learning and Play: Ages 8-12*. She also has been editor of ACEI's *Journal of Research in Childhood Education*.

Elizabeth Deasy earned a BFA from Carnegie Mellon University in Pittsburgh, Pennsylvania, where she taught music, art, and movement to children at Shady Lane early childhood center, the Carnegie Museum of Art, and the Mattress Factory Museum. She currently lives and works in New York City, where she continues her work as an educator and is creating a body of visual artwork and writing an original musical in which she will sing and dance.

Linda Ehrlich, M.Ed. has worked in the field of early care and education for over 20 years. She has directed a school for young children with special needs as well as serving as the director of Shady Lane early childhood center for eight years. She has taught at several Pittsburgh area colleges and is currently teaching a course at Pt. Park University, Integrating the Arts Into the Early Childhood Curriculum. Linda currently works with the Pittsburgh Public Schools as the early childhood programs arts coordinator. She is also President of the Pennsylvania Association for the Education of Young Children.

Debra A. Giambo, Ph.D., is an Associate Professor of English for Speakers of Other Languages (ESOL) in the College of Education at Florida Gulf Coast University in Fort Myers, Florida. She teaches courses in second language acquisition, communication, culture, ESOL methods, and literacy. Her research interests include literacy for English language learners, diversity education, dual language education, and immigrant experiences. Prior to working at the university level, her experiences include teaching PreK-12 students in ESOL, literacy, mathematics, and other areas.

Isabel Killoran is an Associate Professor at the Faculty of Education, York University, Toronto, Canada. She is also associated with the graduate program in Critical Disability Studies at York. Some of the courses she has taught include inclusion at the primary/junior level, curriculum study, human development and socialization, and educating young children. She is an active member of many national and international professional organizations and was the president of the Ontario subdivision of the Division for Early Childhood of the Council for Exceptional Children (DEC). Her interest in inclusion stems from the resistance and frustration she experienced trying to get special education students included while she was a special education and classroom teacher. Her current focus is on preservice and practicing teachers understanding the importance of inclusion and their role in making it a reality. Other research areas include teacher attitudes, preschool/primary inclusion, and adults with intellectual disabilities working as self-advocates.

Sonia Mastrangelo is currently completing her Ph.D. at York University in education, with a focus on parents with children who have autism spectrum disorder. She is working as a research assistant with the Milton and Ethel Harris Research Initiative in the department of psychology, acquiring experience in conducting clinical assessments with parents. She has been a special educator for nine years, both in contained and inclusive environments, for the Dufferin Peel Catholic District School Board. She completed her M.A. at the Ontario

Institute for Studies in Education/University of Toronto in 2001. Mastrangelo currently holds an Ontario Graduate Scholarship and will be teaching her first inclusion course at York University next term.

Carol McNulty is an Assistant Professor in the Watson School of Education at University of North Carolina Wilmington, where she teaches social studies methods. Her research interests include working with teacher candidates (who are largely white, middle-class females) to better serve the needs of students from backgrounds unlike their own. Her work with youth at-risk for delinquency is an important link in this endeavor.

Sandra J. Stone is a professor at Northern Arizona University in Flagstaff, Arizona. She has authored several books and numerous articles, including the books *Playing: A Kid's Curriculum* (GoodYear Books, 1993) and *Creating the Multiage Classroom* (GoodYear Books, 1996). Her interests include play, early childhood, multiage education, and literacy. She directs the National Multiage Institute, which provides professional development opportunities for educators around the world. She also directs the NAU Professional Development School Program for preservice teachers. She is a past editor of ACEI's *Journal of Research in Childhood Education*, and past chair of the ACEI Publications Committee. Stone is a national and international speaker and consultant.

Tunde Szecsi, Ph.D., is an Assistant Professor of Early Childhood Education in the College of Education at Florida Gulf Coast University in Fort Myers, Florida. She teaches courses in early childhood education, diversity, second language acquisition, culture, and ESOL methods. Her research interests include young children's foreign and second language learning, education for young minority children, diversity teacher education, and preservice teachers' cross-cultural awareness and attitude. Prior to working at a U.S. university, her experience included teaching English as a foreign language at the college level and foreign languages and literature at the high school level in Hungary.